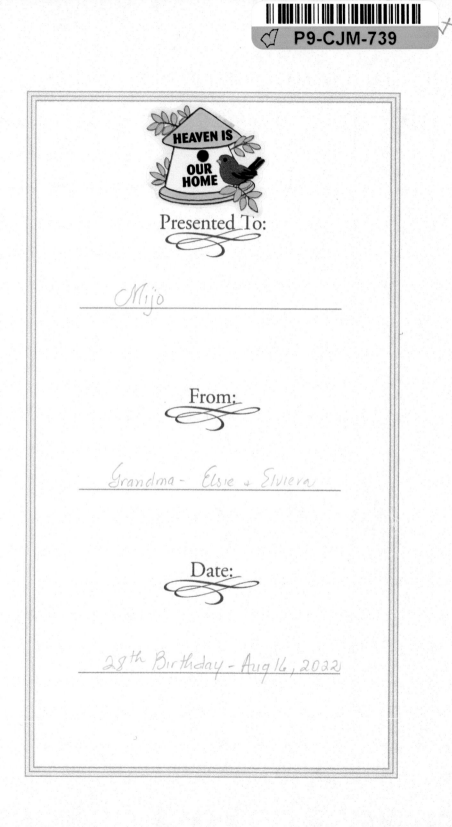

HEAVEN IS OUR HOME

Presented To:

Mijo

From:

Grandma - Elsie + Elviera

Date:

28th Birthday - Aug 16, 2022

DESTINY IMAGE BOOKS BY THOM GARDNER

Healing the Wounded Heart

The Healing Journey

Living the God-Breathed Life

Relentless Love

Altars of the Heart

HEAVEN

an unexpected journey

One Man's Experience with
HEAVEN, ANGELS, & THE AFTERLIFE

JIM WOODFORD
with Dr. Thom Gardner

DESTINY IMAGE® PUBLISHERS, INC.
P.O. Box 310, Shippensburg, PA 17257-0310
"Promoting Inspired Lives."

This book and all other Destiny Image and Destiny Image Fiction books are available at Christian bookstores and distributors worldwide.

Cover design by Eileen Rockwell
Interior design by Terry Clifton

For more information on foreign distributors, call 717-532-3040.
Reach us on the Internet: www.destinyimage.com.

ISBN 13 TP: 978-0-7684-1412-7
ISBN 13 eBook: 978-0-7684-1413-4
ISBN 13 HC: 978-0-7684-1660-2
ISBN 13 LP: 978-0-7684-1661-9

For Worldwide Distribution, Printed in the U.S.A.
13 / 23 22

I dedicate this work to My Constant Friend, my Lord and Master, Jesus Christ for giving me the opportunity to serve His will.

I dedicate this book to my precious wife Lorraine, whose timeless love, endless patience and belief in me I can never repay. I am in awe of the light of Christ in you. I realize now you were my first angel. And to Joey and Jenny for the joy they bring to my life.

To my mother Ruby. Widowed at 22, her love for her children was courageous and beautiful.

Acknowledgments

It is practically impossible to acknowledge and thank everyone who has contributed to the life-changing events before, after, and during the creation of this book. You know who you are and I thank you from the bottom of my heart. I would be remiss, however, if I failed to acknowledge those individuals whose endless love, kindness, and encouragement remind me of Heaven:

- To Pastor Doug and Faith Lamb, my constant friends, for making the journey and this book possible. You are grace and love in human form. Your daughters and their families reflect the love of Christ you give so freely.

- To my sister-in-law Shelly and her husband David Dunphy, for the unfailing love of God I see in each of you.

- To my sisters-in-law Jean McMullen and Karen Pelletier and Jean's son, Matthew McMullen who along with Lorraine, Shelley, and David prayed me back to life. My debt is eternal.

- To first responder and friend, Gerald Rousseau, for his caring assistance to Lorraine in her hour of need, my deepest thanks.

- To Vard and Eileen Gainor whose quiet dignity and wise and timeless counsel reveals the wisdom of a life devoted to God.

- To Pastor Don Lamb of Lifegate Church and his wife Net. Your warmth and friendship brightens my life.

- To Pastor Steve Lindemuth and his wife Danielle and daughter Sami. Danielle, your organizational skills are invaluable to me. Sami, thank you for helping me see my journey through the eyes of a child.

- To Pastor E Daniel Martin of Lifegate Church and his wife Ruth. You are both examples of the goodness of God to me.

- To Pastors Luke and Bonnie Weaver of the Village Lighthouse Church in Benton New Brunswick Canada. After Lorraine, you were among the first of my Constant Friends to hear my story. Your invitation to share for the first time was life changing for me. Thank you sincerely for introducing us to your Godly family of Grace Chapel in Pennsylvania.

- To Pastor Luke Weaver Sr. and his dear wife Edna of Grace Chapel. Over 90 years each of serving God together! Your faithfulness and example is overwhelming.

- To Pastor Mel Weaver and his wife Rosemary of Grace Chapel. Your boundless enthusiasm for Jesus is an encouragement to us all.

- To Irene Weaver Maust Clark and her husband Doctor Grant Clark. Your love and hospitality reflects what I experienced in heaven. And to her recently departed son Jonathan who is now experiencing the glories of Heaven.

- To Pastor Rob Roberge and his wife Tina of Living Hope Assembly for your friendship and interest in my experience.

- To Pastor Ray Hock and his wife Winnie for your interest and support.

- To Pastor Al Frank of Conoy Brethren in Christ Church. Your ready smile reminds me of the happiness in Heaven.

- To Tim Bartholomew, teacher extraordinaire, and his lovely wife Linda for the excitement of letting me tell his Bible students about Heaven. Priceless moments!

- To Maddie Walter and her family. More of my Constant Friends. It is wonderful to see the light of God so bright in one so young. Maddie, you are a blessing to all who come to know you!

- To Amanda Ziegler and Amanda's loving mother Patti Ziegler Wagner. As Amanda lay dying in her mother's arms from an aggressive form of cancer I told her of the beauty of Heaven and its horses. She loved her horse and a look of peace came over her face that was wonderful to behold. It was at that moment I truly realized the power of my experience to give hope and grace to the dying. Amanda, you will never be forgotten. You live on in my story and our hearts until we meet again.

- To Sue and Perley DeMerchant , with whom Lorraine and I had the privilege of being present for the passing of their son Rob to Heaven. He had been injured in an accident and complications sent him into a 17-year coma. Sue and Perley spent thousands of hours at their son's bedside over those many, many years. Never once did they lose faith in God and never once did their love and dedication to their beloved son falter. The closest thing we have on this earth to God's love is a mother's love for her child! From countless hours watching and praying with her son, Sue could tell, despite his comatose state, when Rob was listening. While I sat beside Rob and told him of the beautiful and pain-free Heaven he was about to see, Sue and Perley said Rob was trying to smile in anticipation of his journey to Jesus.

  After his death, so many people came forward to speak of how they would sit quietly with him and sense the grace and peace that came from his silent and motionless body. God speaks to us in so many ways if only we would stop to listen.

  In my soul, I see him running through the green pastures of Heaven with his dog...FREE AT LAST!!!

- To Mr. Alden Kaley, a good friend with a deep love of God, for your friendship, generosity and encouragement on my journey.

SPECIAL MENTION

- **A special thank you to my coauthor Dr. Thom Gardner and his lovely wife Carol. Thom, your deep knowledge of God's word made this a better book and me a better man.**

Contents

Foreword

BY DR. THOM GARDNER

A little while back, I was attending a church conference at a camp in Pennsylvania. There were several hundred people in attendance—some I knew and others I didn't. I like to try to meet folks I don't really know. At the lunch break, I scoured the dining hall to find a new face to sit with when I found two people I didn't recognize. So, I invited myself to sit down along with a friend and a conversation began. The man across from me had a friendly face, and we quickly engaged in a conversation. As we introduced ourselves I asked him where he was from and whether he was a pastor serving a church. The answer came quickly. "No, my name is Jim, and I'm just in the area with a few friends to share my story."

"What kind of story?" I asked.

The man's eyes twinkled at me and he shared, "I was in Heaven for eleven hours and met angels and Jesus." Needless to say, he had gotten my full attention. For the next few minutes my new friend shared his story. I must admit, I am sometimes a bit skeptical of stories such as the one I heard across the lunch table. But this man's story and his manner were warm and genuine. The emotions and tears that flowed as he told his story were real. Over the following days, I met with Jim a few times and neither his story nor his manner changed. It was becoming clear that Jim had a compelling story that would encourage the people of God—a story of transformation and hope.

As a pastor and formational counselor over the past few decades, I have sat at the bedside of folks who were very ill or were passing away. I've held the hands of spouses and children as they let go of the hands of their loved ones to what lay ahead. It has been a mixed experience as many had little to no idea of what was on the other side of the veil.

Jim's story and experience, however, are not limited to those who are passing from this life. Jim's is a story of looking Love in the eyes with resulting transformation. It is a story of the triumph of God's grace through Christ and of Jim's mission as a traveler. Above all, it is a story of the ultimate hope in a life and love coming from the very source of both. Jim's is a story common to many of us who search to fulfill the emptiness of life and who wish to disperse the fears of living. Some feel empty, alone, and abandoned in an increasingly darkened world. It is a message for those whose feet are stuck in the mire of life—those who feel there must be more. Jim's story tells us emphatically that *there is! The Message*, by Eugene Peterson, captures our situation in Ephesians.

> *It wasn't so long ago that you were mired in that old stagnant life of sin. You let the world, which doesn't know the first thing about living, tell you how to live. You filled your lungs with polluted unbelief, and then exhaled disobedience. We all did it, all of us doing what we felt like doing, when we felt like doing it, all of us in the same boat. It's a wonder God didn't lose his temper and do away with the whole lot of us. Instead, immense in mercy and with an incredible love, he embraced us. He took our sin-dead lives and made us alive in Christ. He did all this on his own, with no help from us!*

Then he picked us up and set us down in highest heaven in company with Jesus, our Messiah.[1]

It has been and continues to be my pleasure to get to know my friend and fellow traveler, Jim Woodford. As you read this humble book, I trust that you will be enfolded in the love of Christ as Jim brings his experience and hope of Heaven to you. Be encouraged. There is much more!

---

1 Ephesians 2:1-6, The Message

INTRODUCTION

The Traveler

Let me say at the outset of this story that I am not a pastor. I'm not a preacher nor a Bible scholar. For most of my life I was ignorant or ambivalent about the things of God. The simplest explanation of me is I'm a traveler. I have traveled over the world many times as an airline pilot and businessman. But the journey I'm describing here is far beyond any altitude or speed I've ever flown. I reflect now in these days about the words of a hymn perhaps familiar to you, "Blessed Assurance": "Blessed assurance, Jesus is mine! Oh, what a foretaste of glory divine!"[1] For no reason that I can understand, other than the love and grace of God, I was given that foretaste of glory divine. It remains a mystery to me why that would be so. I pray that the account of Heaven you are about to read may be an assurance for you that Heaven is real, and all of you who accept Jesus as your Savior will see what I saw and more. You will receive more than a foretaste; you will have the entire banquet at His table illuminated only by the light and presence of Jesus Christ Himself, forever!

---

1 Francis J. Crosby, "Blessed Assurance." Public domain.

Each time I retell this account of my experience it humbles me. It was and is miraculous. I reason that what happened to me should have happened to some other person—someone who had dedicated his life to serving God and advancing His cause and kingdom. The only kingdom I had ever advanced was my own. But God invited me into His story. I am living proof that God loves a sinner and will go to any length to bring us to Himself if we accept Him completely. Life seemed pretty good for me and I was enjoying *things*, but never once did I ever have any urge to talk to God, to question Creation, to be involved with anything other than myself. My sole goal was the accumulation of wealth, and I was good at it.

> No matter how many checks I wrote or how many business deals I cut, nothing filled the void. I was empty.

I never thought I was a bad person, but I certainly was not a good person. By all accounts I was a regular guy, no better and no worse than the next person. Oh, sure, I could write a check to a charity of some kind, which was probably also self-serving. My one goal in life was to have *things*. I had a yacht. I had an airplane and a collection of British sport cars. I was an airline pilot and traveled the world. The more I got, the more I wanted. But somehow, no matter how many things I acquired, there was, deep down in my soul, an emptiness and a yearning. No matter how many checks I wrote or how many business deals I cut, nothing filled the void. I was empty.

As you read on, my account may seem fantastic or hard to believe—too good to be true. Nonetheless, it's true. Because of a medical issue, I was without brain activity for 11 hours, and during that time I experienced the glory of Heaven and a glimpse of the roiling darkness of Hell. Though I had flown at more than 30,000 feet in an aircraft many times in my career, I now soared to an altitude beyond the scope of aeronautical instruments to indicate. In a moment, I was transported through a tunnel of brilliant light into fields and pastures surrounding Heaven whose colors and sounds defy description. I looked into the eyes of angels, and yes, I saw the face of Jesus. My experience was not a hallucination, nor was it the result of a drug-induced coma in Intensive Care. It was not the result of deprivation of oxygen. In fact, the medical personnel who attended me were in awe of what happened because for over 11 hours I had no signs of life, no brain waves. Recently, I ran into one of the folks who attended my body medically and heard them call to me, "Hey, Lazarus." For all intents and purposes I was clinically dead. My body was wheeled into a corner out of the way and left on a respirator so that my two children could come from the other side of Canada to say goodbye to me at least in a hospital bed.

Though it may sound strange to folks who believe and serve God, I am envious of you. I had to die to learn what many of you already know and may even take for granted. I had to get hit upside the head with the proverbial two-by-four before I could realize that I was living a life that was empty. I was like a man at a buffet gorging himself on the *things* of life only to never be satisfied. And now I'm living a life that is so full every day. Sometimes my experience in Heaven still seems surreal to me—too good to be true. But it is true. I refer to myself as a traveler because that is what I am. I have traveled the world this side of Heaven at speeds approaching the speed of sound. Now I have traveled at the speed of the light of Christ who sent me back on a mission to share this account and His love.

> I have traveled at the speed of the light of Christ who sent me back on a mission to share this account and His love.

This is my account of an extraordinary experience. I have had some help from my friend, Dr. Thom Gardner, to tell this story. To help you further experience my story, Thom has created a short reflection called "Take the Journey" at the end of each chapter. Take time to experience this reflection and let the Spirit of God draw your heart closer to His.

Take the Journey

As you begin the account of this extraordinary and hope-filled journey to Heaven it is important to fine-tune our compass. To do so, read this Scripture text slowly. Think about these questions to set your hope toward what has been laid up for you in the heart of God.

> *All praise to God, the Father of our Lord Jesus Christ. It is by his great mercy that we have been born again, because God raised Jesus Christ from the dead. Now we live with great expectation, and we have a priceless inheritance—an inheritance that is kept in heaven for you, pure and undefiled, beyond the reach of change and decay. And through your faith, God is protecting you by his power until you receive this salvation, which is ready to be revealed on the last day for all to see.*[2]

Highlight or underline any words or phrases that stand out to you in the verses above. What does the Scripture say about those words? What are your expectations for this life and the next?

---

2 1 Peter 1:3-5, NLT

Notes

CHAPTER ONE

Flying on Empty

My earliest memories are of gazing up at billowy clouds drifting slowly across a northern sky of pristine blue as I lay on my back in the deep snow that covered the landscape around my grandparents' warm and snug home in the province of Newfoundland and Labrador, Canada. For some, this area is known for its long winters and brief summers, and the local joke was that summer was on a Wednesday from 2 to 4 P.M. However, once you visit this unique island you soon realize it should be known for the warmth and friendliness of its people and their legendary hospitality. I read somewhere that difficult terrain and harsh weather forces the inhabitants to develop skill sets and a resilience and friendliness that borders on the remarkable, and that adequately describes the indomitable character of Newfoundlanders. It wasn't until March 31, 1949 that Newfoundland joined Canada, but that spirit of independence and resourcefulness has remained, not unlike the great state of Texas. Up until that time Newfoundland was a British colony and loyalty to the Queen of England is still a proud tradition for many.

During World War II, the island became an important launching area for the United States Air Force and Navy convoys on their way across the Atlantic Ocean to fight the Axis powers in Europe. A number of large American bases were built and thousands of American personnel experienced the charm of its people and the fury of its changeable weather. How ironic that the terrible events of September 11, 2001 would bring thousands of Americans to Newfoundland once again when dozens of passenger jets were forced to land in Gander, NL because all airways over the continental United States were closed to commercial air traffic. Aircraft from all over the world, including dozens from the United States, found safe haven on the tarmac of Gander Airport.

> Little did I realize then that my travels would take me to some of the most exotic locations the earth had to offer and that eventually I would visit the most incredible place of all—*Heaven!*

During the early days of propeller-driven aircraft, Gander was a bustling, busy airport as it was an important refueling stop for airlines crossing the North Atlantic both ways. It wasn't unusual to see movie stars of that era or maharajahs and kings strolling through the airport stretching their legs after the long transatlantic flight. With the introduction of long-range jets, Gander lost much of its international business but still remained an important hub in Atlantic Canada. On 9/11, the town of Gander, NL had a population of approximately 10,400 residents and there were 10,500 stranded passengers in need of help. With love and compassion this little town of Gander and surrounding towns opened their runways, hearts, and homes and for two days took care of every single person without asking or expecting compensation. I am so proud to be a Newfoundlander from Canada.

We lived with my wonderful paternal grandparents. They were as warm as the weather was cold. My dad had passed away when I was two, but God had blessed me with a wonderful mother. As I look back to the sunny slopes of long ago, I realize the love she gave us and the sacrifices she made for us. In those days of the early '50s, especially in the Northeast, there was little in the way of a social safety net for a young widow of 22 with two babies, but she was determined we would never end up in a boys' orphanage. Even though I never really knew my dad, I always missed him. Though my grandad was a great father figure, I couldn't help but notice that I didn't have a dad like the other kids in school or Boy Scouts. The school that I attended was about a three-mile walk from where we lived; I walked it with the cold in my face and the snow crunching under my feet. Behind the school on a hill was the cemetery where my father was buried. I often scaled the hill to where he was placed to rest just inside the gate. I would sit there and pretend he was with me and gaze toward the distant purple hills to the west and tell him of all the places I would visit someday. Little did I realize then that my travels would take me to some of the most exotic locations the earth had to offer and that eventually I would visit the most incredible place of all—*Heaven!*

I can also recall walking home after school through the finger-numbing cold of Newfoundland winters to where my mom and grandmother would have ready a warm bowl of tapioca pudding. That warm house and those loving hands gave me a sense of embrace that warms me even today. There was a hint of Heaven in that tapioca that I didn't recognize at the time.

Logging for the local pulp mill was the main occupation in the central Newfoundland forests, and my grandfather was involved in the business of procuring logs for the mill. Back in the 1950s there were few modern tractors or skidders, so they logged with heavy horses. These gentle giants were a common sight, and many families had teams of horses. The horses dragged the logs on great sleds to locations on the frozen rivers, and in spring the ice melted and the logs drifted downriver to the pulp mill. So I grew up around horses all my childhood. One great advantage of growing up in that cold place with all the horses and the manure—there was a never-ending supply of hockey pucks. And, of course, many Canadian kids are born with a hockey stick in their hands. So I grew up in an atmosphere of hunting and fishing and playing hockey. We also attended a Catholic church, and I experienced Catholic school and the nuns. I was not exactly what you call a devoted follower of Christ; it was just what we had to do. But you know, as remote as the country was, it was my home and I loved it and I still do to this day.

Our family lived at the edge of a river and a large pond. Back then, many small towns were not always accessible by road, so folks got around in the north by small aircraft. There were aircraft on floats in the summer and wheels or skis in the winter. It was great that I grew up in an area where planes would come in bringing in people and provisions and maybe something exciting. For many, those aircraft were our connection with the world.

I was fascinated with aircraft from a very young age. From the roar of the engines to the sight of a float plane skimming the surface of the water to a graceful landing, I was hooked. I did anything I could think of to be around these aircraft. I swept them out or helped with refueling them. I loaded freight in them—anything to be around aircraft and their pilots. I was falling in love with aviation and imagined from a very young age taking the yoke—the control column of the aircraft, if you will—into my hands to take off in one of these big birds and soar through the skies with the grace of an eagle. There was a seemingly endless number of lakes in the north as you can see on any map of the region. These represented new places to go and see. I read everything I could get my hands on about aircraft. I became friends with the pilots and a few of them even took me on flights with them here and there. By the time I was 11 years old, I had my hands on the controls—not alone, of course, but nonetheless it was the most exciting day of my young life.

Like all young boys and girls coming of age I was filled with the thoughts of the endless possibilities that lay before me, but the dream that I held deep within my heart was to become a bush pilot. Although my fascination with aviation was obvious to all, it was a dream that I thought was far beyond the financial ability of my family, and so I quietly resigned myself to *"someday."* Another roadblock was that my grandparents were terrified I would be killed in a plane crash as reports would frequently be heard on the radio that yet another aircraft had been lost in bad weather never to be heard from again. They had lost a young son, my father, and couldn't bear the thought of losing a grandson too.

> It was real flying—a cooperative venture between man, aircraft, and the elements.

In the meantime, my mother had put herself through secretarial school and worked hard to take care of us, and although she never said it, like most mothers she knew the longing in her son's heart. Imagine my disbelief and excitement the evening she sat me down and told me she had managed to borrow the money to send me to *flying school!* Also, my grandparents had relented and agreed I should go on the condition that *I would fly low and slow.* (Bless their hearts, they meant well, but that is probably the most dangerous thing a pilot can do!) I entered flying school and loved it! When I graduated, I was probably one of the youngest commercial pilots in Canada, but because of insurance regulations I had to wait another year before I could fly commercial, so I spent the time loading cargo and soaking up everything I could about the business aspects of flying. At last, the time came for me to fly and be paid for it!

Finally, I could fly on my own. How can I describe what it was like to take the yoke of the aircraft in my hands—to lift tons of steel off the runway or the water? For those moments, it was a feeling of learning to trust myself—of being in control. I could feel the wind around me and learned to fly the aircraft in cooperation with the wind and elements. It felt as though the aircraft was a part of me. I knew what the sky was telling me. In those early days, you really had to fly the aircraft without the aid of computers and fancy electronics. There was no GPS; everything was by dead reckoning—an appropriate term because a simple error in navigation could put you hundreds of miles off course in uncharted wilderness. I especially enjoyed flying the older modified World War II aircraft. In those old airplanes, I could feel the wind on the tail and the resistance of the ailerons (small hinged sections on the wings). It was real flying—a cooperative venture between man, aircraft, and the elements.

Over my flying career, I have flown 42 different types of aircraft. I began flying in an Aeronca Chief on transmission line patrol and then moved up the various types of Cessna float planes and then to the old workhorse of the north, the Noorduyn Norseman. Then on to the Beaver and then to its big cousin the de Havilland Otter and then the twin-engine Otter. From there I was offered a chance to fly a water bomber. I jumped at it! Now here was excitement at its finest as I learned the fine art of fighting raging forest fires with a converted World War II Consolidated PBY Catalina amphibious flying boat known in Canadian service as the Canso.

During the winter, I went south and crop-dusted in Stearman and Grumman Ag Cats and Pawnee aircraft and lived the life of a gypsy pilot. I flew everything I could get my hands on. The days of barnstorming may have been over, but I tasted that rare joy of looking at a new horizon every morning and sleeping under the wing of the aircraft every night. I had the privilege of working with some of the finest old-time aviators, the last of a dying breed. Then came an opportunity to fly a DC-3, and of all the aircraft I have flown, this remains my favorite. For the first time I got to wear a real uniform as a second officer.

People tell me I've led a really interesting life, but to me I was just doing what I loved to do. If one is fortunate enough in this life to make a good living doing something you love to do every day, then you are truly blessed! I managed to get through many scrapes, from mechanical failures to flying through blinding snowstorms, but never once did the passengers in my care fail to safely reach the ground with me at the controls. Some of the best advice I ever got was from my grandfather who told me to keep my head down, my mouth shut, and listen carefully to anyone who had more practical flying experience than I did. I learned so much from those "old eagles" who helped me out many, many times, and I owe them a debt I can never repay.

Eventually, I went to Seattle to train on the 737 jetliners as I had achieved my jet rating. Once I got 2,000 hours in a 737, I took off for England and I flew for a company called Kenting Aviation. I lived outside of London and flew all over the world as a pilot on prop freighters and jets. Times seemed pretty good for a young, energetic jet pilot. I was in control and held the lives of hundreds of souls in my hands as I took hold of the yoke of the aircraft. I accumulated thousands of hours at the controls before I retired.

> I tasted that rare joy of looking at a new horizon every morning and sleeping under the wing of the aircraft every night.

So, I had a seemingly interesting and fun life, but the last thing on my mind was God. We would fly through the day into night and land somewhere exotic. At the time, I was single, the stewardesses were beautiful, and I was interested.

I can recall flying over the South China Sea, looking up from my instruments into the inky blackness of the sky that was perforated with countless stars that seemed to fall into the boundary where the sky ended and the sea began. You might assume I would have had the presence of mind to suppose there could be someone responsible for all this, maybe a Creator. But in my arrogance, I could not see beyond that empty darkness. Yet subtly, permeating undefined darkness was an awareness that there must be something more than this.

I was enjoying *things*, but never once did I have any urge to talk to God, to question Creation, to be involved with anything other than myself. My sole goal was the accumulation of wealth, and I was good at it, having invested in several business opportunities. Yet there would be in the background a sense of emptiness and longing for something more. I dismissed it, thinking that it meant that I needed a new plane, a new boat, a new Jaguar, so I'd go out and buy it and play with it for two or three days and still the yearning would come back.

One of God's saving graces was meeting my precious wife, Lorraine. Toward the end of my flying career, I was on horseback riding in the country on a frozen river. As I rode through the cold, steam blasting from my horse's nostrils, I saw a beautiful woman also on horseback. That seemingly chance meeting on the snow was destiny calling, and she altered the course of my life.

> Though I had flown to the greatest heights in a powerful jetliner to see the actual curvature of the earth, I didn't understand that there was something more. Much more.

I was good to my family. I provided everything I could for them. Lorraine came from a different spiritual background than I did. While I attended the Catholic church out of tradition and obligation, Lorraine had a deep relationship with Jesus Christ. She and her sisters always had a strong Christian upbringing. But when Lorraine and her sisters went to church, I went away or went out on the boat or flying. I was polite but never wanted anything to do with all of that "church business." To be honest, I thought my sister-in-law, Shelly, was naïve when she spoke of trusting in Jesus for everything. She and her husband, David, were two of those people who saw the hand of God in everything. They were filled with joy. I reasoned that for intelligent people, some religious guy had done a real selling job on them. Shelly was warmth and kindness personified and a really great cook on top of that, but she and Lorraine had a joy and depth beyond my understanding. Never once did I ever question where these two amazing ladies' faith came from.

Though I was surrounded by the goodness of God, I never saw it. From the love of my wonderful mother to the warmth of my grandparents' home and the love of my wife Lorraine, I didn't see or acknowledge much besides the routine of life. Life was one more *thing* to be had. Though I had flown to the greatest heights in a powerful jetliner to see the actual curvature of the earth, I didn't understand that there was something more. Much more.

Take the Journey

Many of us have a sense of the futility of life—that life is an endless pursuit of something more than what we have or know. Even those who have strong faith find that their relationship with the One who breathed them alive vacillates between the miraculous and mundane. There is a search to find something to fill us—the grass always seems greener somewhere else. Our favorite experience is the next experience. It seems as though we drive a new car off the lot and we notice another, more desirable car before we get to the next stop sign. Yet there *is* something more—much more for us. The longing in our hearts comes from the One who longs for us.

> The longing in our hearts comes from the One who longs for us.

Take a few minutes to connect with this longing in the heart of God to know you and for you to know and experience Him. Read the words of Isaiah slowly to yourself.

> *Therefore, the Lord longs to be gracious to you, and therefore*
> *He waits on high to have compassion on you. For the Lord is*
> *a God of justice; how blessed are all those who long for Him.*[1]

Highlight any words or phrases that stand out to you. What do you think about the truth that the Lord longs for you to be connected to Him? Does this feel true for you personally? Are there other ways in which you have tried to fill some emptiness in your life? Things? Relationships? There is a blessing for those who long for the presence of God in their lives.

---

1 Isaiah 30:18

For Further Reflection

Our hearts long for a home and rest. This longing and seeking in our hearts is like a GPS, a "God Positioning System," which tells us how close or far we are from home. Sometimes we make a wrong turn in our search to fill this longing, but this GPS programmed by the mercy and longing of a Father's heart recalculates and vectors us toward home again.[2]

Now, envision yourself in the very throne room of Heaven standing before Jesus. As you stand with Him, ask Jesus to reveal His longing for you to know Him in greater depth. As He makes His longing heart known, sit in quiet focus on the face of Jesus.

Prayer

Holy and gracious Father. I long to know You face to face. I confess that I have tried to satisfy my heart with lesser things that fall short of Your presence in my life. I ask You to reveal to me anything that I have pursued to fill this longing in my heart that You alone can fulfill. I quiet my heart now to listen to Your Spirit. Amen.

---

2 Thom Gardner, *Living the God-Breathed Life: An Invitation to Rest at the Table* (Shippensburg, PA: Destiny Image, 2010), 28.

Notes

CHAPTER TWO

Out of Control

I am bent over and racked with pain. All day long I walk around filled with grief. A raging fever burns within me, and my health is broken. I am exhausted and completely crushed. My groans come from an anguished heart.[1]

Have you ever woken up in the morning having slept in a funny position that left your arm kind of numb and tingly? It feels as though you've been injected with Novocain or some other agent. You can't do anything with your arm until the feeling returns, which usually happens rather quickly. It's weird when you tell your arm to do something and it doesn't listen to you.

One morning I woke up and both arms and both legs felt numb and tingling. Previously, if I had woken up with an arm that had gone numb

---

1 Psalm 38:6-8, NLT

I could shake it off and the feeling would return quickly. But something was seriously wrong on this particular morning a few years back. It was a strange feeling. I began to question myself—what had I done? How could my sleep position have resulted in this kind of numbness of all my extremities?

A few hours later, I was feeling very ill and got sicker as the day went on. Like a typical guy, I thought this sensation would just go away. It didn't. Maybe I had a bug of some kind. This was on a Sunday. When the sickness didn't go away by Monday, I went to the doctor. He examined me and, I thought, confirmed my diagnosis—that I had the flu. I returned home to wait out the sickness, but it didn't leave. I returned to the doctor a few days later and he assured me it was flu and that it would wear off. But it was becoming obvious that something was very wrong. I was in the grip of something more sinister. I was getting weaker by the day.

On day ten I returned again to the doctor. This time I collapsed in the parking lot of the doctor's office. Some kind person dragged me into the office. Lorraine, a nurse, insisted that this was not the flu and that I see a neurologist. I had gotten the doctor's full attention, and they finally brought in a neurologist for a deeper look. The neurologist ordered a lumbar puncture to extract some spinal fluid. The doctor returned with the results of the tests they ordered, and I could tell something was seriously wrong by the look on his face. He said, "At first when you presented clinically, we thought you had multiple sclerosis," which in itself is not good. "But the tests revealed that you have a very rare disease, which is why it would have been difficult for your doctor to diagnose your illness. You have contracted Guillain-Barré."

This disease was very rare. It was named after the two French doctors, Dr. Guillian and Dr. Barré, who first isolated the disease in Paris in the '40s. With this disease, your own autoimmune system attacks your body. It destroys the myelin sheath on the brain stem—a kind of insulation covering the bundle of nerves. The myelin sheath allows the proper functioning of nervous system. When the myelin is damaged, nerve impulses slow down and the nerve cell begins to wither. It is like a gang of electrical wires woven together that lose their insulation and begin to short one another out. MS can also result from damaged myelin sheaths. This was perhaps why the doctor originally believed I had MS. The myelin sheath around my brain stem was tattered and torn. My nervous system was out of control.

The prognosis for this rare disease was grim. If it is diagnosed within short period of days, the treatment is a plasmapheresis—a blood purification procedure and intravenous immunoglobulin. This removes the problem but may result in a period of paralysis. Recovery is possible, but with lingering effects. However, if the disease isn't identified within that narrow window, it may result in an ascending paralysis beginning with the legs and moving up the body to paralyze your lungs. The end of the disease may be death. As I said—grim.

> But like everything and every other time in my life, I thought I could be in control.

There is very little medical investigation put into Guillain-Barré because it is so rare a disease. Those who have it simply have to learn to live with it.

While the doctor was explaining the disease to me, he spoke words that brought me to a chilling hopelessness: "Jim, it's too late for you. You've missed that window of opportunity, and I'm afraid that you are condemned to a lifetime of pain." But in my arrogance I thought, *It can't be that bad. I'll fix it.* At that moment, I should have fallen down on my knees and prayed to God for help. But like everything and every other time in my life, I thought I could be in control. In any event, the doctors tried plasmapheresis. This was done several times in an effort to ease or eradicate the virus from my body that was causing the disease. Despite their best attempts at treatment, I ended up with some measure of paralysis. My fingers started to curl, so they taped sticks to my fingers to keep them straight. I went from being someone who was once in control of a high-powered aircraft to someone who couldn't even wash my own face. I couldn't do anything without the help of a nurse or a nurse's aide or Lorraine, my wife. Finally, my life and body were out of my control. I could not throttle past this one. I had been in many scrapes before, with engines failing or even times when I dove my water bombing aircraft straight into a forest fire. But there was no controlling this catastrophe. My life was to be in a downward spiral. I was humbled and helpless and, worse yet, dependent upon other people, which was an unfamiliar feeling for me.

When I got out of the hospital and went home, I did my best to follow the doctor's orders. I was a mess, I really was. Even to get out of bed was a painful ordeal. I would have to roll out of bed on my hands and knees and crawl up the dresser and then have someone help me. Again, I felt as helpless as a toddler. It was awful. In order to manage the disease, I had physiotherapy with the doctors trying all kinds of neurological drugs. I even had private hyperbaric chamber treatments for healing and pain management. But nothing stopped the pain. My nervous system was like a bunch of electrical wires and circuits without the insulation, all short-circuiting at once. Every impulse from my brain to move my hands or feet or, in some cases, even blinking my eyes resulted in pain. I'm not talking inconvenient pain or nuisance pain. I'm talking soul-searching, gut-wrenching, screaming out in the middle of the night pain. In the very bad times I had to move into another bedroom for fear of keeping Lorraine awake. I kept a leather belt by my bed to bite down on when the pain was intense in order to keep from screaming in the middle of the night. I never knew pain like that existed. The torment was a constant hell on earth.

> I kept a leather belt by my bed to bite down on when the pain was intense in order to keep from screaming in the middle of the night.

The paralysis and pain effected all of my life, even the way I walked. Along with Guillain-Barré comes foot dragging, so when I would walk my right foot dragged behind me.

The pain would get worse, with occasional deceptive times when the pain would subside a bit only to return with a vengeance. I could tell when a relapse and pain were coming on, but I never prayed. I just bit down harder and muscled through the onset. I never prayed. This became a new reality of life for Lorraine and me. My speech was slurred. I couldn't swallow anything but liquids for a long time, but I forced myself to do the exercises to be able to get around a bit. Eventually, and with great help and effort, I was able to teach my body to walk again.

I thought to myself, *Oh, these are the cards I've been dealt. I've had a good run up until now.* Most pilots are pragmatic people because we deal with the reality of keeping an airplane in the sky. You learn to live with whatever the skies bring. You try, and if it fails, you crash—so be it.

I was out of my mind with pain. The doctors ultimately prescribed powerful narcotics to deal with my constant, life-altering pain. This was a strange experience for me. Because of my love of flying, I never really drank alcohol or took drugs of any kind. The strongest thing I took was an aspirin. I would not do anything that might endanger the career that I loved. Nonetheless, they put me on narcotics. The drugs made the pain manageable so that I could live and function. They didn't take away the pain, but they dulled it. With the medication, for the first time I had something that would allow me to drift off to sleep instead of lying awake in pain for several hours. But it seemed that the more of that stuff I took, the more I needed to maintain a level of manageability. Soon, I regret to say, I began to lie to Lorraine. She would ask whether I took my medication, but in fact I was sometimes taking

> I was headed down a fatal path. In a short time, things would get deadly serious.

three times as much to have some sort of ability to function. I was headed down a fatal path. In a short time, things would get deadly serious.

One afternoon I got a call from a surveying company regarding some land markers they asked me to approve. Late that afternoon, I crawled into my pickup truck and drove up to the property. I came to the crest of the hill and, for a moment, was taken by the image of the golden setting sun. I parked the truck and I sat there for a few minutes getting up the nerve to move my body and bracing for another wave of pain that would surely come.

I crawled out of the truck, holding on to the side to keep from falling. I saw a length of drainage pipe in the box. I reached for it and thought how easy it would be to attach this to the tailpipe and just go to sleep and just end the pain. I had come to the final destination on a long road of desperation. I was thinking of killing myself—to just go quietly into the darkness. And yet, something deep inside of me revolted against this ultimate surrender, and instead I climbed back into the truck. I realize now that God must have changed my train of thought.

While I was bracing myself for the pain, I looked down and saw a full container of my pain medication in the console of the truck. I didn't realize that over the months of taking these strong drugs I had built up a tolerance and a toxicity in my body. There was an irony to sitting in my truck watching the beautiful sunset while at the same time being tormented in pain. I was looking for peace. So, I reasoned, if I took a few more maybe they would stop the pain. I was growing weak and weary in the battle against the pain and paralysis of my disease. I was not trying to kill myself; I was trying to kill the unrelenting pain.

I remember sitting in my truck and looking at the setting sun and swallowing several pills. I found out later, after my experience, that the bottle of opioids was almost empty. I had tried everything possible under the sun to get some sort of relief and I couldn't find it unless I took these narcotics. My mind was on not wanting to be a bother to anyone and maybe trying to find some kind of control over my pain. Again, I was my own last resort. My only hope was in myself and in the drugs.

Suddenly, having ingested many pills, instead of relief I began to feel a different kind of sensation. The bottom of my feet began to burn, and the burning rose up my legs and then up my thighs involving the entire lower part of my body. Something was terribly wrong—I had done something catastrophically bad. My body was shutting down. It was as though the cab of my truck was filling up with water and I was drowning, gasping for air. I was dying...I was alone.

Take the Journey

I am bent over and racked with pain. All day long I walk around filled with grief. A raging fever burns within me, and my health is broken. I am exhausted and completely crushed. My groans come from an anguished heart.[2]

When we are in pain, it engulfs us. When we are in pain, we slide into self-preservation mode. The pain controls us, our families, and everyone's lives revolve around that pain. We live in desperation to stop it. It is as though we are in the dark; we see nothing but the ever-present pain.

People in physical pain are in a desperate search for any means of relief. People caught in the pain of life lose vision and therefore are desperate for hope. The psalmist goes on to say, "You know what I long for, Lord; you hear my every sigh. My heart beats wildly, my strength fails, and I am going blind."[3] When we are in pain we cannot see the future; we only see the sameness of the moment and feel trapped.

> It was as though the cab of my truck was filling up with water and I was drowning, gasping for air. I was dying…I was alone.

But in the darkness of pain there is also silence, and it is in the silence that, if we can listen, we hear the voice of God. The darkness and hopelessness brings an end to our natural ability. Billy Graham once said, "When we come to the end of ourselves, we come to the beginning of God."[4] In the dark we try to see with natural eyes. We flail against the darkness and hopelessness. We feel as though we are alone in our pain, whether physical or the pain of life.

---

2 Psalm 38:6-8, NLT
3 Psalm 38:9-10, NLT
4 Billy Graham, *Hope for a Troubled Heart* (Nashville, TN: Thomas Nelson, 1991), Chapter 11.

Further Reflection

There was a man in the Old Testament, a prophet of God mighty in deeds, defeating and dispatching false prophets in a power encounter on a hilltop. Though he had done mighty things for God, he succumbed to the lies of the enemy and ran away in fear until he came to a cave. The cave was a place of darkness where natural vision had to cease. Now there were earthquakes, winds, and fire.

"Lord, is that You?" Elijah said in his raised, quivering voice. But no reply came forth. Then the earthquake was joined by a fire from Heaven, like the fire Elijah himself had called down only days before. "Is that You—Lord?!" Elijah's voice now raised to a shout. "Is that You?" Nothing. He put his hands over his ears to shut out the deafening sounds. When the natural and supernatural disturbances were at their peak—when it seemed that it could not get any louder—a sound began to seep through the bluster. It was faint, but as definite as the sound of a single violin playing a high sustained note above the din of a full orchestra. The sound seemed to grow, not louder, but more prominent as it continued. Eventually it was transformed into a breathy whisper that seemed to distract all of Elijah's attention from the storm—so much so that it caused him to stand up, uncover his ears, and step into the mouth of the cave to hear it better. It was as if the storm of his inner turmoil was being engulfed—embraced—in softness. The sound, as it drowned out the storm, was like that sound he had heard a hundred mothers utter to their crying babies. It was as though Elijah heard the sound of God's voice gently whispering, "Shhhhhh, Elijah. It will be okay. I am here...I am here...Shhhhhhh."[5]

You are not alone!

Consider your own journey through life and any areas that seem beyond your control. They may be in a relationship, physical illness, or finances. Perhaps you are in a cave of fear or despair. You've come to the end of your natural vision and ability to see your way through or manage your circumstances or pain, whether physical or emotional. You have come to the end of yourself. You may feel trapped as Jim was or as Elijah who came to a cave on the mountain of God.

Yet in this place of darkness, the Lord wants to reveal Himself to you afresh. Let's stop for a moment and take a deep breath. Quiet your heart and mind the best you can. Enter into the cave with Elijah. Are there mighty winds or earth quaking under your feet dislodging you from your securities of life—the things you've always counted on? Maybe these are your natural abilities or talents or material resources. Where do you feel trapped as Jim was? Read Psalm 38:6-8 again. Pause and consider any words or phrases that stand out to you. Are you wracked with some kind of pain? Are you grieving over a loss or a relationship or perhaps your health? Have you come to the end of yourself? Take time in the presence of God to allow the tumult and confusion to settle down and listen for the sound of the gentle stilling. Shhhhh. You are not alone.

---

5 Thom Gardner, *Healing the Wounded Heart: Overcoming Obstacles to Intimacy with God* (Shippensburg, PA: Destiny Image, 2005), 96-97.

Notes

CHAPTER THREE

Poised Between
Heaven and Hell

For He rescued us from the domain of darkness, and
transferred us to the kingdom of His beloved Son, in
whom we have redemption, the forgiveness of sins.[1]

As the sun was slowly setting on the day and my life, an impulse arose—
an involuntarily dawning from deep within me. For the first time in my
life, I tried to raise my arms to the setting sun. A force greater than myself
was arising from a place I never acknowledged throughout my entire life.
Some awakening spiritual instinct erupted into words—whether I said
them out loud or not is unclear to me. These were the first three of six
words that would carry me into the presence of God. But I raised my

---

1 Colossians 1:13-14

hand and I said, "God, forgive me." The last thing I remember is slumping over and hitting my head on the steering wheel.

I don't know how long I was there bent over the steering wheel, but I leaned back and sat up straight again. The burning was gone. I could see. I felt really good. In fact, I felt terrific! I thought, *Wow, that medication really worked*. Feeling rejuvenated, I got out of the truck and walked about 15 feet away. I felt as though some kind of heavy, wet garment had been taken off of me leaving me light and alive.

Feeling more alive than I had for a long time, I turned and looked back at the truck and saw that the truck door was closed, though I did not remember closing it. As I looked closer, it appeared that there was a body slumped over the steering wheel. The head was turned toward me, and I saw blood coming from the mouth. At that moment, I became angry at the thought that someone was in my truck. What or who was this? I was filled with anger and rage! Who would dare to get in my truck without my permission and have the nerve to fall asleep? In my rage, I started toward the truck to open the door and give this person a piece of my mind. My indignation was overwhelming.

> I raised my hand and I said, "God, forgive me."

Have you ever had a dream where you tried to walk or run but it seemed as though your feet wouldn't or couldn't move? Instead of a step I could only manage a few inches with great difficulty. The more I struggled to move, the more resistance I felt. As I looked down at my feet it seemed as though I was looking through my shoes, and I could see the ground beneath them. I suppose I must have just thought it was the result of the medication I had taken. I tried to move forward again, and ever so slowly I inched closer to the truck. I can't begin to describe my fright and amazement because the truck door was closed and locked from the inside. I looked a little more closely and realized, *It's me!* I was somehow outside of my physical body. But I could see, I could feel—I had all of my faculties but no pain of any kind. What was this? How could this be? Was I dreaming?

As I stood looking on in astonishment, a million thoughts ran through my mind. No sooner had I begun to try to get my bearings then I had the sensation I was beginning to rise. Now, as a pilot I'm a good judge of altitude. In seconds, I was above and looking down on the bed of the truck. Then I was 1,500 feet up and then 2,000 feet and rising faster and faster.

I could look down and see my feet, but when I looked up I saw the tunnel of light that I have learned many who have had near-death experiences have reported. A golden circle about 60 feet in diameter appeared; the center swung inward, revealing an entrance to an immense distance. As I looked up at it, it opened up, and I began to pick up speed and slipped right into the tunnel. It was like being a kid remembering the first time I went down a tunnel slide. I slipped over the edge and into the tunnel. But this was not on a schoolyard; this was a tunnel of light. As a pilot, I'm also a good judge of air speed, yet there was no kind of wind or buffeting like flying those old aircraft into the forest fires in my water bombing days. It felt as though I was going a minimum of one thousand miles an hour, yet totally silent and, again, with no sensation of wind. My being was tilted backward at about a 45-degree angle, traveling feet first inside this tunnel of light. Inside the tunnel there was what I could only describe as a swirling cloud on the inside, but more solid than cloud.

> A golden circle about 60 feet in diameter appeared; the center swung inward, revealing an entrance to an immense distance.

Again, I had full cognition, being fully aware of where I was and having my mind and senses. As I was rocketing along, I sensed a focused light at the end of the tunnel. There was an air of expectancy woven together with terror. Still, conscious of the overdose of medication I had taken, I thought to myself, *Now you've done it. What's at the end of the tunnel?* I was unaccustomed to being taken where I didn't want to go. Here, in this unexpected journey toward the light that I was approaching at tremendous speed, I was once again out of control. This isn't like losing an engine over the ocean; this is the big deal—the real deal. I was not holding the yoke of an aircraft this time. The arrogance of control and command in my life was intoxicating. Many pilots are known for it. This was an entirely new sensation for me.

A Soft Landing

Suddenly, my lightning travel through the tunnel began to decelerate and I knew something momentous was about to happen. As I drew closer to the end of the tunnel, the opening was getting wider, and I decelerated from blazing speed to a gentle, soft landing standing upright again. I was standing before the light at the end (or exit) of the tunnel. It was covered with a mist, but it was obviously a portal and I knew I had to step through. Before me was a verdant landscape brilliant with light. As anyone would do stepping into an unfamiliar place, I carefully put my foot out and looked down to see that I was standing on the most incredibly beautiful, perfectly manicured green grass anyone could ever imagine. (Maybe that is what is meant when people say, "The grass is always greener on the other side.") To my amazement, when I put my foot on the grass, light rippled out from under my foot. Light was everywhere.

> Now the dismal atmosphere reverberated with the screeching sound of Hell's gates that cut through me and filled me with a soul-shuddering terror.

Right and Left, Heaven or the Abyss

Upon taking my second step onto the grass, the tunnel vanished behind me. Before me, it appeared as though someone had drawn a line—a median line separating right and left. To the right, brilliant yet soft light filtered through a subtle mist. But to the left, the ground sloped downward and away sharply into a crevasse of deep blackness. The walls of this crevasse were of a black, glistening, coal-like texture. Now the dismal atmosphere reverberated with the screeching sound of Hell's gates that cut through me and filled me with a soul-shuddering terror.

As I looked to the left and down, the steep slope disappeared into a mass of roiling, boiling black clouds. It was like looking in a clothes dryer filled with clothes turning over and over again. It was dark and rolling rapidly up the slope as if coming to overtake me. From this roiling blackness came a sickness and awful smell—a stench of death, hopelessness, and of things long dead. The darkness boiled toward me faster and faster. This black, massive, shape-shifting cloud to my left was filled with a dark and clammy presence permeating a deep murkiness. The darkness held a damp chill devoid of life and warmth. It seemed to me as though I was standing on the cusp of the rotting mouth of Hell and evil. Out of this darkness climbed a creature of gruesome description, and I knew it was coming for me. Its eyes focused on me and glowed like burning coals. It opened its hideous mouth and I was mesmerized by the horror of the saliva dripping from its fangs. It was hungry for my soul.

As I looked to my right in desperation, the scenery couldn't have been more different. All of us at one time or another have gotten up early on a summer's morning to find a beautiful mist hanging over the trees and the fields. We pilots call it "ground effect." Dewdrops cover the grass, and there is the promise of another beautiful day. While we may not clearly see the sun, we know that it's there illuminating and filling the shimmery morning mist. As I stood at the meridian between Heaven and Hell, I instinctively turned toward the right and into the light.

Whispers from the Darkness

As I turned toward the light, I could hear murmuring of dark voices coming out of this dank fog. At first, the voices were muffled and unclear as though I was hearing words spoken in the next room through a thin wall. I couldn't make out what they were saying, but there were multiple unrecognizable voices—whispers from the darkness. I turned away and toward the right and the luminescent landscape as the sinister voices became more clear and insistent. The voices spoke with a hissing quality directly to me as though a serpent were speaking to me, inviting me into the pit. I began to perceive the voices saying, "Jim. Jim. Jim! Jim! Quick, come this way. Over here Jim. Come with us—come with us."

> I felt the sharp scraping of a claw or talon going down the back of my shoulder.

Now I really began to tremble. I tried to turn away from the pit and toward the light. But the more I turned away from the pit and the voices, the louder and more insistent was their tone. Added to the dread invitation was a physical attack. I felt the sharp scraping of a claw or talon going down the back of my shoulder. All the while the voices grew louder, the taunting invitation more desperate, "Jim, come with us. We're here for you! This is where you belong!" The voices seemed to be filled with a strange, gleeful excitement, anticipating some dreadful event.

The more I turned toward the light, the more the darkness tried to draw me into its foul stench. With the sharp claw in my back and the screeching of demonic voices around me, I felt as though evil would have me. When my soul's freedom was under assault, these words erupted from the same deep place as when I said, *"God forgive me"* in my pickup truck. I cried out, *"God help me!"* Six words filled with power.

The instant I spoke these words, the light on my right side became brighter, the darkness immediately retreated to the crevasse about a hundred feet back, and the voices stopped. The tone of my words was pleading, begging, and coming from a place of total powerlessness. There was nothing in me that could have evaded the appalling doom of that dark pit. I did belong there. My life had been all about me. Now I was beseeching God for help. *Beseech* is a word we don't use much anymore. It was a helpless and beggarly request. "God, help me!" I was out of options. To my wonderment, and in the midst of my despair, God answered my desperate plea.

Points of Light

The instant I cried out to God, three points of light appeared from behind that bright mist on my right as though my cry had cued their arising—as though they were waiting and watching over me. They appeared like the arising of the morning star that appears shortly before dawn, which has been used as a point of reckoning for navigation from ancient times. At first, these points of light were distant and formless, rapidly moving toward me from three different positions and converging on me. There was one light at probably 40 degrees, another at about 180 degrees, and another one about 270 degrees. The faster they came toward me, the brighter they became. As the points of light approached my position, their light intensified and flooded over and beyond me and struck the creature out of the darkness. As the

> When my soul's freedom was under assault, these words erupted from the same deep place as when I said, *"God forgive me"* in my pickup truck. I cried out, *"God help me!"* Six words filled with power.

glowing light struck the creature and the darkness, it shrieked and roared in pain. The creature and the stench that permeated it recoiled violently and scrambled back down the crevasse, disappearing into the darkness like a rat scrambling for a hole! The evil could not abide in the approaching light. Darkness and evil cannot exist in the light of *God!*

I had stared into the abyss—into the very mouth of Hell, nearly caught in its pernicious pursuit of my soul. Now these three lights were increasing in size, coming toward me at a tremendous speed and taking on an awesome form. Someone had heard me, and I had the feeling that this was a search and rescue party coming for me. As the three lights grew closer, they began to take on a brilliant and glorious form. The terror and blackness of the pit was being replaced by wonder and excitement. My heart leapt for joy as three lights became three distinct forms.

Take the Journey

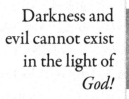

Have you ever been put in a position where you felt helpless—dragged away or overwhelmed by a power you could do nothing about? God, the source of all light and life, sees us in our battles with the darkness of sin and self-effort. Sometimes we are in over our heads and need a rescue party to come looking for us.

Of all the attributes of God we need to remember that He is heroic—that He comes to our rescue. We are locked up in the tower of the evil one, and Jesus arrives on a white stallion to save us. From the first chapters of human history in the Bible, God is a rescuing champion. He rescued an entire nation from the clutches of the enemy by opening the Red Sea right before their eyes. The people escaped certain death or captivity and the enemy was destroyed, chariots and all. When we were locked in sin and self-effort, Jesus Christ came riding over the hill on a white horse with His banner—love unfurled in the breeze. He is a Hero.

> Darkness and evil cannot exist in the light of *God!*

There are precious promises to those whose feet are ensnared in the darkness—when we find ourselves at the edge of the darkness. It has little to do with us and more about the reality of the heroic salvation in Christ, our Hero Messiah! Listen to the words of the apostle Paul as he described our rescue:

> *For He rescued us from the domain of darkness, and transferred us to the kingdom of His beloved Son, in whom we have redemption, the forgiveness of sins.*[2]

---

2 Colossians 1:13-14

Think about the struggles you have. Where does the darkness call your name? Where do you feel overwhelmed? What do you hear the words of the Scriptures inviting you to do? Take a few moments to meditate on the invitation of God. As the light of God moves toward you, let it overwhelm you as you watch the darkness scramble back into the pit.

For Further Reflection

In order for the rescue party to come, we must recognize our need to be rescued. We, in a similar way to Jim, may be standing at the edge of darkness alone. Note that God always makes the first move toward us. He loves us and rescues us out of His own nature, which is love. Jesus is the Hero of the story who saw us in our lostness at the edge of the pit. He saw the claws of Hell as they tried to pull us into the darkness. He waited for us to call for help, knowing we could not make it on our own. Christ, the Hero, was not motivated to rescue us by our eloquence of speech or accumulated good deeds but solely on the basis of His own nature, which is love. Read and reflect on these words.

> God makes the first move toward us in mercy. It's a kind of romantic love, really. He knows the dark towers of sin and separation we are locked up in and sets out to rescue us. He is willing to get His hands dirty, as He did at first when He picked up that dust and breathed into it. In mercy God came to rescue us from ourselves. The same breathy love that created us is the very thing that allows us to be with Him.[3]

Simply put, Christ the Hero rescued us because we needed to be rescued. The only requirement is that we realize that need and call out to Him as Jim did: "God forgive me—God help me." As we call out to Jesus, our Rescuer, He calls us not only to rescue us from eternal destruction

---

3 Thom Gardner, *Relentless Love: Unfolding God's Passion, Presence, and Glory* (Shippensburg, PA: Destiny Image, 2012), 50.

but into a new life filled with power and wonder. He has called us out of darkness and into the light of His presence in the now-ness of God. And as He brings us into the light of His presence, we live in that light here and now this side of Heaven.

> But you are a chosen race, a royal priesthood, a holy nation, a people for God's own possession, so that you may proclaim the excellencies of Him who has called you out of darkness into His marvelous light.[4]

Prayer

My gracious Hero, Lord Jesus Christ, I thank You for seeing me at the edge of darkness. I recognize that I cannot rescue myself. I call out to You now and ask You to be my Hero. In Jim's words, "God help me—God forgive me." By Your mercy, bring me into the light of Your presence to live there always moment by moment. Thank You for being my Hero. Amen.

---

4 1 Peter 2:9

Notes

CHAPTER FOUR

The Face of Angels

What are people that you should think about them, mere
mortals that you should care for them? Yet you made
them only a little lower than God and crowned them
with glory and honor. You gave them charge of everything
you made, putting all things under their authority.[1]

As I watched the three lights converging on my position at tremendous speed, a new concern occurred to me based on my long-acquired piloting instincts. I began to be concerned that they might need to put on some flap to slow down for a safe and proper landing. Just habit, I guess. As the three lights began to take on form, I realized they were more than points of light coming out of the distance. These were not some kind of UFOs. They were angels! I watched in wonder as they came to a soft,

---

1 Psalm 8:4-6

perfect touchdown right in front of me. Before me stood three indescribably beautiful creatures. If I could only paint what my mind's eye saw! The creatures displayed brilliant colors beyond the palette of any artist to reproduce.

How can I explain these indescribable beings? Earthly words fail me. The three angels glided toward me making no sound of any kind, though their movement created a rippling wake illuminated with a pure light.

> In that moment, I knew that God had heard my plea, "God help me." I fell to my knees overwhelmed with awe and gratitude on the soft green grass of Heaven.

The angels were not all identical; each one was slightly different from the next. The first angel closest to me was about ten feet tall! I was taken by the beauty of his face and regal bearing. His features were perfect and his face gleamed with the love of God. The second angel, about 12 feet tall, caused me to open my eyes even wider in awe. He, like the first, was clothed in a simple garment woven more of light than a fabric. Now the other two moved aside and the third and tallest angel stood before me about 15 feet tall. He was dressed somewhat differently than the other two who preceded him. (Note that I say "he" but their gender was neither distinct nor important.) This one was clearly in command holding a greater authority. These three were magnificent angels—glorious representatives of the light and love of Heaven's throne.

In that moment, I knew that God had heard my plea, "God help me." I fell to my knees overwhelmed with awe and gratitude on the soft green grass of Heaven. The heavenly light rippled along the ground under my bent knees, flowing toward and blending with the brilliant light of the three angels before me. While much of their appearance was similar to what we recognize about angels, there were also many facets that I will try to describe.

Imagine a face that is neither male nor female, that carries the best of both genders. Faces most incredibly regal and majestic, with very light, brilliant hair and a luminescence of holiness shining from within—the very light of God. They were dressed in the most elegant white robes. I use the color white to describe their faces, hair, and robes, but it was more than a color; it was a fullness of glory that has nothing to do with color. Color is an inadequate term to describe the appearance of these beings wrapped in radiating brilliance.

Now the three angels moved and began to glide toward me. I stood to my feet, and instinctively I reached out my hand as if to touch the reality of their presence. As I reached out, the smallest angel came around beside me. (Small is a relative term; he was ten feet tall.) As I was marveling at this brilliant and shining being so close to me, he reached back to me placing his hand on my arm as if to reassure and connect with me. His hand rested lightly but warmly upon my forearm for a moment. And then he spoke without words to my heart, saying, *"Fear not, James, we are your constant friends."* This was no chance encounter with three angels whose turn came up in the angel rotation that day. I now understood that they had been assigned to me since my birth! The touch of the angel's hand on my arm sent a warm feeling of assurance and comfort through me— body, soul, and spirit. As his arm encircled my shoulders I felt as though I was being hugged by 50 grandmothers simultaneously with a hint of tapioca. (I actually smelled tapioca.) It reminded me of the comfort I felt as a small boy coming in the door of my grandparents' house on a cold winter's day to be greeted by my mother and grandmother with that warm, comforting smell of tapioca pudding. It was such a warm and comforting thought that God, in His infinite care and compassion, knew that my first glimpse and experience of Heaven would be so overwhelming that He put before me things that I loved as a child to calm my heart. Heaven was beginning to feel more familiar, like home to me.

The angels I experienced didn't have wings with feathers in the way artists may have portrayed them in a painting. Rather, I saw that they had two spires of golden light coming up from the back of their shoulders that radiated a light, making their heads shine. This created an effect above their heads resembling a halo. What we see as a halo is the radiance of the spires of their wings of golden light creating an arc of gold above their bodies.

Perhaps the most astounding aspect of the appearance of all three of these angels was their eyes. They were the deepest violet, a blend of colors describable and indescribable—colors of both Heaven and earth. These eyes conveyed a regal calm that was as deep in love and compassion as they were in color, moving me to feel as though I was the only person who had ever been born. And those wondrous eyes never blinked!

> As his arm encircled my shoulders I felt as though I was being hugged by 50 grandmothers simultaneously with a hint of tapioca. (I actually smelled tapioca.)

The Warrior Angel

There was, among the three impressive beings, one who literally stood head and shoulders above the other two. As I mentioned earlier, he stood about 15 feet tall with garments that were slightly different. He was not only larger, but clearly had a commanding presence—more gravitas. His garments were more distinct and regal, and as he moved toward me the light of his robe rippled like moonlight on water. The other two angels deferred to him, bowing slightly and moving out of the way as he approached. His apparel was subtly different in that his garment was brighter than that of the other two. The hem on the sleeves of his garment was also gold with threads of purple running through it embroidered with intricate and beautiful detail.

Upon his garment and over his shoulder was a sash of gold and a belt of the same color around the middle of the garment. There were a few notable details that set him apart as the one in charge. This one wore a scabbard at his side. I cannot say that I saw a sword in the manner we might expect in the scabbard, but there was what appeared to be an instrument or weapon composed of purest, brightest light. (Maybe George Lucas, creator of *Star Wars,* had an angelic encounter that inspired the lightsaber.) The form of the scabbarded weapon was beyond my experience and ability to describe. The best I could offer was that it was a sword of light. He had a medallion around his neck—I later learned it was called a gorget and was shaped like a crescent moon laid horizontal. This was a piece of battle armor such as warriors would wear in ancient times to protect the throat area. This piece was engraved with letters of some kind from another language I could not decipher, but the markings appeared to shimmer as if alive! This commanding angel had come prepared to do battle with the darkness that had threatened me, and he had won.

> Perhaps the most astounding aspect of the appearance of all three of these angels was their eyes. They were the deepest violet, a blend of colors describable and indescribable— colors of both Heaven and earth.

The warrior angel approached me and I felt dwarfed by his physical stature as he looked downward toward me. All at once, to my great astonishment, the angel deferred to by the others now bowed to me—to me! How could this be? I esteem myself as the lowest of the low—a mere lowly man. I was not a holy man of God who had spent one minute pursuing Him or even giving Him the time of day. I cannot accurately portray my feelings at this moment suspended in eternity. This amazing being filled with the light and perfections of God bowed to me! Who am I?

I felt quite small by comparison to the immense stature of the warrior angel. Then he began to speak, not as you and I might speak. His mouth didn't move, nor was there an audible voice. Rather, there was a communication or thought transference of spirit to spirit. I knew what he was saying as his thoughts entered my own mind. The communication was on a deeper level than earthly, audible words could express. His communication surpassed mere language as if coming from someone who knew me very well. It was not unlike the connection some married couples experience after years of being together who know each other so well that one hears the heart of the other and might even finish their sentences. (Some might find that irritating.) Yet, the spiritual tone of this innate voice was both rhythmic and calming. His thoughts resonated in me. His communication seemed to be formed simply, yet with a kind of Victorian propriety or gentility.

With my heart becoming settled in the presence of this heavenly encounter, a question arose from my own heart. I asked the angel, "How could you bow to me? You who live here in this place, in the presence of God."

> I cannot accurately portray my feelings at this moment suspended in eternity. This amazing being filled with the light and perfections of God bowed to me! Who am I?

What I heard next humbled me beyond description. *"James,"* he said, *"man was created by the very breath of God. The light of God's essence is in you. That light becomes tarnished with sin and turning away from God. But the light is still in you and all of mankind. When we bow to you, we are honoring the light of God in you."* I began to understand that these powerful, majestic beings were in awe of us—of mortal man. The same light that lit up the garden of Heaven and that filled the angels was in me! What moved the angel to bow to me was not anything about me; it was the light of God. The host of Heaven is in awe of us. We are precious and unique beyond our mortal comprehension.

Everything around me in Heaven was filled with light, from angels to flowers and even the grass on which I stood. The question "Who am I?" was being answered in a most unexpected way. I am simply one who God heard crying out for forgiveness and help. I am one for whom God banished the darkness back into the pit of Hell. I had not yet seen a small fraction of the wonders I would be shown, each one more amazing than the last.

Take the Journey

It's difficult for humans to truly comprehend their standing before God. We often forget that we were created by and for the love of God. Maybe you've asked yourself the same question Jim asked of himself: "Who am I?" Or maybe something like, "What does God see in me?" The answer to that question is as simple as it is transforming. What God sees in you is Himself! We are much more than the sum of the physical stuff we are made of. With the joys and challenges of everyday living we sometimes lose sight of who we are or who God has made us to be. Listen to the words of the psalmist:

> The question "Who am I?" was being answered in a most unexpected way. I am simply one who God heard crying out for forgiveness and help.

What are people that you should think about them, mere mortals that you should care for them? Yet you made them only a little lower than God and crowned them with glory and honor. You gave them charge of everything you made, putting all things under their authority.[2]

It seems the psalmist asked the same kind of question. "What are people? As Jim stated in his story, the angels are in awe of us somehow. They know something about us that we need to know; we carry the very breath of God! That breath was knocked out of us when man gave in to the temptation of the serpent in Eden. Let's make this personal—you were created by the breath of God. You were created to carry His light as bright as the angels Jim encountered. You were created with free will, able to choose your own way. Look at the words of the psalmist a little more carefully.

---

2 Psalm 8:4-6, NLT

You were crowned with the very glory and honor of God. You have eternal value. You were created to rule over the works of creation with tremendous authority. It was for you that the Father sent His Son, Jesus, to rescue you from the darkness if you would only call out to Him. You are the one seated with Christ as the apostle Paul wrote:

> *But God, being rich in mercy, because of His great love with which He loved us, even when we were dead in our transgressions, made us alive together with Christ (by grace you have been saved), and raised us up with Him, and seated us with Him in the heavenly places in Christ Jesus, so that in the ages to come He might show the surpassing riches of His grace in kindness toward us in Christ Jesus.*[3]

When we don't know or experience our true nature and identity in God, we can get discouraged and try to fill our emptiness with things—try to create an identity for ourselves separate from God. You were created to carry the light of God through Christ. You were created to live and reign with Christ.

Further Reflection

Take a few minutes and read the following paragraph concerning your true nature and identity.

> From the moment we drew His first breath, the Eternal could not take His eyes off of us. We took His breath away! Beloved, God is a personal God who created us in His own eternal breath for the most intimate communion with Him. Imagine this: the very first conscious awareness of Adam was of being kissed alive by the Creator. We are the Artist's rendition of Himself—His handprints were still fresh on us.

---

3 Ephesians 2:4-7

He knew every contour of our form and every thought in our hearts. Can you envision with me that when Adam met with God in the cool of the day (see Gen. 3:8), the very breath of God who formed him welled up in him and was exhaled back to Him in praise; "Hhhhhhaallelujah."[4]

Take a few minutes and reflect on this paragraph. Quiet yourself as best you can, casting off the cares and self-talk of the day. As you become settled notice the breath going in and out of your lungs. Can you imagine that this is the very breath of God you're inhaling and exhaling? Allow the breath to go deep inside of you to find any place of weariness or self-doubt. You are the Artist's rendition of Himself. You carry His light and love. Angels bow to you. Angels have been assigned to you since birth. You carry an eternal weight of glory.

Prayer

Heavenly Father, I ask Your forgiveness for forgetting Your breath within me. I ask that You help me to live with the conscious awareness of Your breath. I give You any judging or critical words I've spoken about myself or other people. I thank You that You have crowned me with glory. I thank You that You made me to reign with Your Son, Jesus. I thank You that I am seated together with Jesus and that the darkness had been placed under my feet. Now I give You honor and praise by returning Your breath to You—hallelujah! Amen.

---

4 Gardner, *Relentless Love*, 48.

Notes

CHAPTER FIVE

Walking with Angels

*And the city has no need of sun or moon, for the glory of
God illuminates the city, and the Lamb is its light. The
nations will walk in its light, and the kings of the world
will enter the city in all their glory. Its gates will never
be closed at the end of day because there is no night there.
And all the nations will bring their glory and honor into
the city. Nothing evil will be allowed to enter, nor anyone
who practices shameful idolatry and dishonesty—but only
those whose names are written in the Lamb's Book of Life.*[1]

What is Heaven like? Heaven is like the earth, but ten thousand times
ten thousand more beautiful and serene. The most grandiose vistas and
scenery on earth are only vague hints of the beauty God has prepared for

---

1 Revelation 21:23-27, NLT

us in Paradise. The most unexpected aspect of Heaven's landscape was that colors had sound and sounds had color, creating a sensory spectrum that overwhelmed my being with a sense of wonder.

Again, the commanding angel bowed to me in a gesture of invitation, saying, *"Would you walk with us?"* I nodded my head in acceptance. Then the angel turned gracefully and gestured with his arm the direction he wanted me to go. Now, with an angel on either side of me and the tall angel directly behind, they began to usher me into a landscape of unimaginable beauty. I was forgetting the tunnel and the pit that lay behind me and was totally present to those who attended my way.

IMAX Vision

Heaven is not a globe or sphere, so there is no disappearing horizon in the landscape. Heaven is a continuous panorama expanding to infinity in every direction. Yet I could see features right in front of me with great clarity. It was as if the concept of distance was expelled from Heaven and eternity. Heaven exists in a spiritual dimension beyond our terrestrial experience. Things like colors, time, relative size, and distances are finite terms that are not really useful for describing the infinite nature of Heaven.

As I was walking along the pathway with the angels, there was a great augmentation of my ability to see not only what was before me but also in every direction at once. There was full peripheral vision on all sides, behind, and before without turning my head in any direction. It was more of a panoramic awareness. I'm at a loss to explain the level of clarity and awareness in Heaven. We see everything here in this life in mostly a surface, two-dimensional perspective. The vision in Heaven allowed me to see at greater depth. There was 360 degrees of vision that I can only compare to being in an IMAX theater with no limitation in depth or distance. It was as though I could see the single bloom of a flower on the side of a distant mountain, yet also see those sights directly in front of me at the same time. My eyes became as a microscope and telephoto lens simultaneously.

The Landscape of Heaven

Heaven's landscape was punctuated with recognizable features like the appearance of mountains, trees, flora of all kinds, streams and brooks filled with brilliant blue, crystal water. All of the features of the surrounding landscape were filled with a bedazzling array of colors and sounds beyond any artist's palette or composer's manuscript, all laid out in a multi-sensory banquet under a brilliant blue yet sunless sky. In my estimation, the blue was a deeper blue than I was used to seeing in the sky. Not darker—deeper.

As we walked along, this simple woodland path surrounded with lush green grass appeared before me. Simple may not be the best description, as in fact it was a path of breathtaking, variegated color. There were blooms of flowers of dizzying variety bordering the path on both sides. Trees bedecked with iridescent leaves hung over the surrounding landscape we were walking through. I was on sensory overload and had to pause to take in the scenery with the angels on either side of me. They stopped to allow me to absorb what I was seeing. As I looked down at the flowers along the path, I was confused at first. It looked to me as though the flowers were all one mass of color. But I discovered, as I bent down, that the petals of every flower were translucent, like stained glass. The flowers were pearlescent. Each flower's color merged with the color of the next, one beneath the

> The petals of every flower were translucent, like stained glass. The flowers were pearlescent. Each flower's color merged with the color of the next, one beneath the other.

other. There would be a red flower and beneath it was a yellow flower and then a blue flower and then the green with the stem. The appearance of the flowers reminded me of multi-faceted stained glass of every color melded together providing shades of known and yet indescribable varieties of colors and colors merging with other colors. I stopped to study them a little more closely. One of the angels saw that I was obviously transfixed and overwhelmed by the wonder of the flowers and smiled in delight. As we moved along slowly, the angels pointed out various aspects of this indescribable flora.

The flowers not only had color; they had sound as well. Accompanying the visual beauty was a concert of impromptu music created by the petals of the flowers as they were moved by the constant, gentle breeze that filled the landscape. There was a sense that the flowers sang an original and infinitely flowing melody without cadence or conclusion. I said to the Guardian, "Is that music?"

> The tall warrior angel described joy as living on the edge of a huge laugh motivated by a constant awareness of the presence of God.

He said, *"Yes, James, the flowers and all of Heaven are so happy you're here. They are filled with joy. They are singing to you."* To me! The tall warrior angel described joy as living on the edge of a huge laugh motivated by a constant awareness of the presence of God. I cannot help but smile thinking about that definition. I experience that feeling even today as I recall my experience in Heaven.

There were also brooks or small streams of water there about three to four feet wide. They were not deep. The water was a brilliant blue. The pebbles that lay on the bed of the streams were golden in color. The water was lit from the bed of the stream with light ascending upward as rivulets of light danced on the surface of the stream. The water made sound as well. These streams also composed a spontaneous, tinkling musical offering that accompanied our steps through the landscape. The angel described these streams as the "living water of life." I was told that these brooks fed into a larger central river that flowed beneath the sixth gate of joy into the city of Heaven. Every stream was connected to every other stream just as we are to one another. The flowers, the breeze, and even the streams all sang together creating a symphonic concert that resounded throughout Heaven's landscape, flowing and cascading to the throne of God.

As I continued to examine the flowers, I bent toward them and the most wonderful fragrance came up from them. Like everything else I experienced in the garden of Heaven, I strain to compare it to what we have on earth. The fragrance could be compared to a memory of being surrounded by sweet-smelling jasmine flowers I experienced in the South Pacific or perhaps the smell of the incense burned during the Catholic mass I recall as a small boy. It was sweet and powerful in effect, yet not overpowering. It was the pervasive fragrance of love that permeated everything around me in Heaven. It was a scent that filled my senses and flowed along with the breeze. I turned to the angel on my left and I said, "They smell so beautiful."

The angel said, *"Yes, James, that is the scent of sanctity."*

Everything in Heaven reflects the love and nature of God, from the colors upon colors to the fragrance of the flowers to the constant serenade of music to the startling purity of the streams of water flowing through Heaven. The city itself is illuminated by the very presence of God. No sun nor moon nor stars—only the light of God and the Lamb. All things, every sensory input, inspired by and bearing the signature of God.

Eternal Light of Heaven

As a pilot for many years, I was first trained to orient my geographical position by use of the greater and lesser lights in the heavens. To my great surprise, there was no source of natural light in Heaven. There was no sun, no moon, no stars or other celestial source. Everything, and I mean everything, was infused and bursting with the light of God. Light comes out of everything—from the grass and the flowers to the angels. Absolutely everything is filled with light and there is *no darkness at all!* Because light came from everything, there were no shadows. But imagine for a moment looking at scenery and there are no shadows of any kind. Everything in Heaven was revealed in a dazzling optical clarity. There is also no shadow of doubt or disbelief, no shadow of shame, no shadow of death. This all-pervading light is like the light of truth that banishes any shadow of falsity. There is no need for shade or shelter from a blazing sun because there is no sun. There is no need to hide from foul weather in Heaven. There is no weather. The light felt like the warm and gentle love of God. I can imagine that Heaven is rather like the Garden of Eden. Physically, the temperature was like a constant 72 degrees.

> Everything, and I mean everything, was infused and bursting with the light of God. Light comes out of everything—from the grass and the flowers to the angels.

As I have shared this experience here and there, I have been asked, "Well, weren't you allowed a period of rest in Heaven?" That would assume that somehow I was weary or tired. The simple answer is that it was not necessary like it is here on earth with all of our cares and worries and physical limitations. I was unaware of any pain or distress or fatigue of any kind. In fact, the only emotion carried to the precincts of Heaven is love. To my awareness, my body was more a blend of spirit and flesh and therefore there was no weariness or physical fatigue, yet I could move as I did in my earthly body.

Although I was not weary, there were along the pathway little alcoves or areas where one might pause for a meditative reflection—nests of quiet focus as a person might do at twilight or the end of a full day. These spaces were softly snuggled in the green and variegated flora and filled with the music of Heaven's joyful greeting. Yet there is no end of the day and eternal light in Heaven. There is rest in the embrace of Heaven's loving light.

Enthralled, I gathered in the sights and sounds of Heaven's landscape that spread out before and around me in every direction. As we walked along we came to a large meadow in the midst of Heaven's garden. It was bordered by a familiar sight that had been with me on earth for most of my life—a sight that was a delight to me and that made me feel as though Heaven and this precinct of paradise was created just for me. There were horses in Heaven!

> This precinct of paradise was created just for me. There were horses in Heaven!

Take the Journey

And the city has no need of sun or moon, for the glory of God illuminates the city, and the Lamb is its light. The nations will walk in its light, and the kings of the world will enter the city in all their glory. Its gates will never be closed at the end of day because there is no night there. And all the nations will bring their glory and honor into the city. Nothing evil will be allowed to enter, nor anyone who practices shameful idolatry and dishonesty—but only those whose names are written in the Lamb's Book of Life.[2]

Jim's account of Heaven is filled with the word *light*. Light seems to be in everything, from the angels to the grass. There was no darkness of any sort in Heaven. The Scriptures tell us that, "God is light, and in Him there is no darkness at all."[3] In truth, the presence of God is not reserved for Heaven alone. His love surrounds you even as you read these words. In the light of His loving presence there is no shadow or fear or shame or doubt. There is only the longing of God's heart to walk with you as He did with Adam in the garden in the breeze of the day. I can imagine that before the earth was fallen into corruption, perhaps the brooks and flowers also sang.

Imagine walking through life, through your daily living surrounded and bathed in the light of God as Jim experienced, where every step and every moment held a new wonder to be taken in. In fact, the world we live in here and now could be a preview of Heaven as we turn attention toward God and away from all the stuff that distracts us. While we are here on earth we can learn to be mindful and present to the wonders that surround us now.

---

2 Revelation 21:23-27, NLT
3 1 John 1:5

For Further Reflection

At the same time, the throng of Heaven sang a continuous antiphonal praise to the holiness and glory of the One who dwelt in unapproachable light. The atmosphere around the throne was filled with the sweet scent of something like cassia and cinnamon. It was a vision of utter purity and light, enthroned and filling every sense and beyond.[4]

Take a minute and consider that at this moment the One who created you desires to have you come out of the shadows and live in the light of His presence. He is calling you "out of darkness into His marvelous light."[5] Out of the shadows of doubt and disbelief, out of the shadows of shame, out of the shadows of death itself. He is establishing His throne room even now in you.

Let's take a few minutes and come out of the shadows. Quiet your heart the best you can. Sit for a moment and take note of the breath going in and out of your body being refreshed moment by moment. Now, become aware of the sounds around you. Sounds of nature—even sounds of the normal activity of life. All of nature can clearly testify of the presence and nature of God. The apostle Paul said, "For since the creation of the world His invisible attributes, His eternal power and divine nature, have been clearly seen, being understood through what has been made."[6]

Now, listen carefully. Acknowledge that Heaven is orchestrating the sounds around you. As you sit in God's presence, allow yourself to be bathed in the light of God. Put on His presence as a garment, as Adam and Eve were clothed in the light of His presence before the fall. Now sit surrounded and bathed in the light of God's presence and allow the warmth of God's love to clothe you as you sit in His presence.

---

4 Gardner, *Relentless Love*, 97.

5 1 Peter 2:9-10

6 Romans 1:20

Prayer

Gracious Lord. Help me to be aware of Your presence even here and now on earth. Help me to walk with You as You did with Adam and Eve. Let me walk in the light of the Lamb of God. Let me discover the wonders You have placed around me even in this flawed and fallen world. With this prayer, I put on Christ. Amen.

Notes

CHAPTER SIX

The Sticky Love of God

*Long ago the Lord said to Israel: "I have loved
you, my people, with an everlasting love. With
unfailing love I have drawn you to myself."*[1]

As I walked along with the angels, bedazzled by Heaven's pathway, I became more aware of the love of God with each step. God was so merciful and kind to me knowing the traumatic experiences that preceded my excursion of Heaven's wonders. He was aware of the experiences of passing out of my mortal body and the drabness of earth and moving at light speed through the tunnel. He was aware of the sensory overload of Heaven's kaleidoscopic landscape. But more than that, God was aware of all that had happened to me from the first moments of my life. He knew my attempts to master my own life to my lack of an earthly father. Heaven

---

1 Jeremiah 31:3, NLT

was a reflection of the love and heart of God. Revelations of the extent of His kindness grew more personal and touching. Literally.

At one point walking along the pathway, moved by the patience and hospitality of the angels, I reached out to take the hand of the commanding angel as you might do with any friend. The intimate nature of God's love and compassion was revealed to me with what happened next. To my great delight, when I touched the angel I was aware of a warm sensation that pervaded my entire being. I didn't feel as though I'd crossed over a boundary of heavenly propriety. The experience is difficult to put into earthly words. It was more than a physical warmth; it was a feeling of home. Curiously, when I withdrew my hand, the light of the angel's body clung to my hand. It was as though the love of God this awesome angelic figure carried was sticking to me. God loves us with a sticky love! Love clung to me and hinted that it wanted to draw me back into itself. Love wanted me—to reclaim any part of me that was disjoined from it. It was a love that knew me better than I knew myself—a love that loved me more than I loved myself. I stood there as the light clung to my hand; looking at my hand; looking at the angel; looking at the elastic, sticky love of God. I finally let go and this light of love rebounded into the arm of the angel. The expression on the angel's face was as one who had introduced me to a precious moment for the first time. God was so kind, so hospitable, so aware of my heart. The feeling of delight connected me to the angel and the angel to me. I long for that connection even now.

God is so kind that He again placed something in front of me that comforted me amidst the emotional roller coaster of my passing. As we walked along, we approached a slight rise along the pathway. At the crest

> When I withdrew my hand, the light of the angel's body clung to my hand. It was as though the love of God this awesome angelic figure carried was sticking to me. God loves us with a sticky love!

of the rise we came to a split-rail fence as on our horse farm in New Brunswick, Canada. The tallest angel motioned to me with his hand causing the sleeve of his garment to fall back slightly. I heard the angel's voice say, *"James, look."*

I followed his gaze into this pasture filled with lush green grass that glistened as it was moved by the constant slight breeze. Now trotting over from the midst of this idyllic scene were three of the most beautiful horses I have ever seen. One of the horses was pure white and looked like Silver, the Lone Ranger's horse. He seemed the most willing to connect with me. There was another one that was kind of a bay in color. Then there was a palomino. All three animals were the pinnacle of their breed, and all were also immaculately groomed. I was thrilled and warmed. What better way could Heaven have made me feel at home than to bring me to a pasture with beautiful horses that have been such a big part of my life. They reminded me of the stunning white Arabian horse that carried my wife, Lorraine, to our very first meeting on that frozen river. I had always been around horses, and no matter where I flew in the world or wherever I lived, from Canada to my time in England, I've always owned and loved horses. Horses were more than pets to me; they were a connection with something powerful yet personal, from their familiar smell to their power and yet their ability to respond to the slightest nudge in direction. They are faithful and ask no questions. They are just there with grace and nobility.

Now the warrior angel made a little motion with his hand, and the horses' heads came up and instantly they were at the fence. I don't know who God appoints to look after horses in Heaven, but they were beautifully groomed, seeming to emanate the light of Heaven. I would be glad to do their care when I take up residence there. As the horses moved across the pasture, the grass under their feet sparkled. It was surreal. The three beauties came right up to me at the fence with the white one leading the way. I'm sure that my face erupted in a smile at their approach.

I once read that a horse is nobility without conceit, friendship without envy, and beauty without vanity, a willing servant, but never a slave. If only people were like horses!

As I gazed into their shining eyes, I felt they knew of my lifelong love for their kind and they were now returning that love a thousandfold. I put my hand through the fence and the white horse nuzzled my hand and stepped closer with a greeting nicker as if he was saying, "It's good to see you." I moved my hand across his graceful neck and began to stroke his stunning coat. It was like putting my hand in silken light. A wonderful feeling ran through my hand and arm, like when I touched the angel. The most amazing thing was that again, as I withdrew my hand, the light that was in the horse clung to me until it was about six inches away and then returned to the coat of this glorious creature. This was the same as when I touched the angel. Another example of the sticky love of God that was once more flowing over me even from these magnificent animals. There aren't enough superlatives to describe these animals in the glimmering pastures of Heaven. They were exquisite and I was captivated.

> As I withdrew my hand, the light that was in the horse clung to me until it was about six inches away and then returned to the coat of this glorious creature.

Once again, God and the host of Heaven showed me incredible and generous hospitality by bringing me to horses in a pasture. God wanted me to be comfortable as I adjusted to the light in Heaven. It was like coming out of the darkness of my earthly life to the brilliance of Heaven's love-inspired warmth. How good is God!

I saw horses in Heaven, but no people whom I knew. I have been asked since my experience in Heaven whether I saw any of my family who had passed on. I did not. I didn't see my grandmother or grandfather, both of whom I loved dearly, or my father, whom I loved but never really knew. I will see them all upon my next arrival in Heaven as they died in faith. The reason may be that the angels knew I was not going to be staying. For others, family members may meet those who are taking up residence in Heaven as their eternal home.

Contrails of Prayer

As I stood in this beautiful landscape of Heaven, my pilot's instincts tried to get my bearings and configure the beautiful blue sky of Heaven. But there were no lights, stars, suns, or moons. Note that the vault of Heaven and the horizon are unique in that the expanse goes on for eternity with no effect of distance. I was trying to orient myself in the sunless sky. In my many years navigating earth's sky in the cockpit, I had acquired an inner compass to find direction and geographical orientation. But now my confused inner compass asked, "Am I northeast? Am I southwest?" But I was still in earth mode.

Then, as I scanned the vault of Heaven I spotted something like streaks of brilliant light going straight up. They appeared to my pilot's mind as contrails as I might have seen in earth's skies behind an aircraft. Contrails are the water vapor in the exhaust of jet engines that become frozen into crystals in the stratosphere. They appear as thin streaks of cloud to us on earth. But these contrails in Heaven were very different. They were more brilliant and appeared to paint the sky of Heaven as vertical streaks, not horizontal as I might have seen on earth. And besides, there are no aircraft in Heaven.

I looked at the warrior angel and pointed upward, asking, "What are those?"

His reply brought me to tears. *"James, those are the prayers of your family for your soul. They are coming up to Heaven before God even now."*

They were contrails of prayer. In the blaze of Heaven's glory, I had almost forgotten my earthly life. I learned later that when Lorraine was told what had happened to me, that I was beyond hope, she and her sisters

Shelly, Jean, and Karen; my brother-in-law, David; and Jean's son, Matthew gathered in our home to pray in a prayer circle. There were six in the prayer circle and there were six contrails of prayer coming up to Heaven. They were led to pray that the Lord would send me back. It seems the group was praying in agreement with what God had already decided to do. Our faithful petitions to God paint the vault of Heaven as contrails of prayer coming up before God as we pray.

With a gentle look of reproach in those beautiful violet eyes, the angel told me that, sadly, mankind is losing the will to pray. He said we have become on earth a culture of instantaneous gratification. With our so-called advances in technology, communication is now at our finger tips, and we want everything now. Without thought of consequence, we pray to God for some request on Sunday and if it doesn't appear by Tuesday, we think God doesn't care or isn't listening. That is simply not true. God hears our every petition, and in fact it is recorded and noted in the halls of knowledge. Our grandparents and ancestors knew the power, value, and importance of prayer. After a hard day's labor, they would gather with the family at eventide to read the Bible, meditate on the Word of God, and in that restful time also pray.

> Our faithful petitions to God paint the vault of Heaven as contrails of prayer coming up before God as we pray.

Today, after a busy day when we have a few quiet minutes we text, Facebook, or call each other. There's nothing wrong with that, but we need to remember that those rare quiet moments are in our busy lives and orchestrated by God. As if He is saying, "I am here, My child; tell Me about your day, and I will put it in order and give you peace that passes all understanding." If you want proof that prayer works, pray for someone else and watch what happens. God loves a selfless prayer. God loves "knee-mail."

God's love lights everything in Heaven. God's love is sticky, emanating from everything from angels to horses in Heaven's pastures drawing us to the heart of God. Our prayers, motivated by that same love, ascend to Heaven in contrails of prayer finding their way to the throne of God. I will share more later of the nature of prayer coming up to Heaven. Prayer is always heard in Heaven—prayer is never forgotten.

Now as I turned again toward the angel, the landscape around opened to me once again, and I saw the magnificent city—the city of Heaven.

Take the Journey

Long ago the Lord said to Israel: "I have loved you, my people, with an everlasting love. With unfailing love I have drawn you to myself."[2]

God loves us with a "sticky love." It is everlasting. It does not grow weary or wear out. Love wants to draw us back to Himself—a love that draws us deeper into the heart of God. This love, as described in the Scriptures, is an everlasting, eternal love with no beginning and no end. We bandy the word *love* around a lot these days. We love some kind of food or we love someone who does something for us. We may say we love the weather. But the love of God flows from His very nature. John says, "God is love."[3]

Before we were born, God made up His mind to love us. We were created *in* love to *be* loved. Yes, we stumble and fall short of God's love and glory, yet He picks us up again and brings us to Himself. Even when life seems unfair—when others abandon us—our faces appear before a gracious Father in Heaven. "For my father and my mother have forsaken me, but the Lord will take me up."[4]

As Jim shared from his experience in Heaven, the love of God draws us into connection with Him. God's sticky, elastic love draws us back to Himself. Jim shared that the love of God stuck to him and also remained with him. Another amazing thing was the hospitality and compassion that characterized God's attitude toward Jim. Remember that Jim had done nothing to serve God up until that point. It is, however, safe to say that the love of God Jim experienced in Heaven has had a profound effect on him and has changed his life.

2 Jeremiah 31:3, NLT
3 1 John 4:8,16
4 Psalm 27:10

Another moving aspect of God's love is that it makes a home for us. Or maybe we could say that it makes us feel at home even in this world where we are strangers and aliens. Consider the kindness of God that greeted Jim with tapioca and horses in Heaven. How precious.

Take a minute now and slowly read the paragraph below, aloud if possible.

Further Reflection

To be loved of God is to be the reflection of His very nature. He is love, as the Scriptures say. The single most irrevocable and important statement within our resume is that we are loved by God! This is the greatest thing about us. The love of the Father started in His heart and moved out toward us with no thought of the worthiness of its object. There is no *because* in the love of God for us. We can lay aside all of the reasons God loves us personally and intimately.[5]

Now allow yourself to get as quiet as you can. Take in a deep and relaxing breath and reflect on this chapter and the paragraph you've just read. Turn aside the cares of the day, whether the day is behind you or ahead. Be present in this moment. Perhaps you disqualify yourself from the love of God or people. Maybe you believe you have not done enough. The greatest item on your résumé is not what you have done but that you are loved simply for being you. In humility we must add that we can only love God because He first loved us.[6] Allow yourself to be touched by the sticky love of God right now as you read these words.

---

5 Gardner, *Relentless Love*, 62.
6 1 John 4:19

Prayer

Gracious God and Father—I thank You that Your love for me does not depend on what I do or give or how I look. I reach out to You at this moment and believe that Your sticky love will cling to me and draw me to You. I thank You, Jesus, for sticky love. I thank You that in Your sticky love there is no "because." Amen.

Notes

CHAPTER SEVEN

The City of Heaven

That you, being rooted and grounded in love, may
be able to comprehend with all the saints what is the
breadth and length and height and depth, and to
know the love of Christ which surpasses knowledge,
that you may be filled up to all the fullness of God.[1]

Seeing my family and friends praying for me from Heaven's view penetrated my heart with the reality of their love for me. As I was enraptured by this humbling outpouring of love, I felt a gentle tug on my elbow. I turned to see the 13-foot angel looking at me with those brilliant violet eyes. The silent wonder of the moment was interrupted by words communicated by this angel, saying, *"James, look."* He purposely waved his arm causing the sleeve of his robe to move back and a huge, perfectly circular reflecting pool appeared before me. At first, I thought it was a flat pane

---

1 Ephesians 3:17-19

of glass until the angel subtly motioned with his hand causing a ripple to move across the surface of the pool.

In a moment, I was somehow, I can't explain how, above and looking down on the City of Heaven. I was gaining an aerial view much like I would have had as a pilot while on approach to a city or in a holding pattern. I was surveying the heart of the city in all its glorious splendor. The walls surrounding the holy city were remarkably thick as though nothing could possibly prevail against them. I was told that, in fact, the stunningly beautiful countryside was referred to as paradise or "walled garden." An overview of the city unfolded before me as we would occasionally swoop in for a close-up on particular aspects of the city, and with my enhanced vision I was able to see everything. What I observed resembled a huge parkland with buildings that didn't intrude into the landscape but rather melded in with the beauty of it.

> In a moment, I was somehow, I can't explain how, above and looking down on the City of Heaven. I was gaining an aerial view much like I would have had as a pilot while on approach to a city or in a holding pattern.

The city of Heaven was immense. I didn't actually walk the streets of Heaven, but I was given something like a high-definition virtual tour in infinite yet intimate detail. I will try to describe my view of the city of Heaven from the highest altitude to my descending to street level, so to speak.

From the highest point the city of Heaven appeared to me as a group of several massive concentric circles of golden boulevards separated by other circles of lush greenways. It was interspersed here and there with cascades of sparkling crystal waterfalls with softly meandering waterways. The streets were not the brassy gold color of earth, but a gold with all impurities removed, resulting in a softer, muted tone. Overlaid upon this immense group of circles alternating from gold to green were cross-shaped intersections. Within these immense circles, smaller walkways and buildings could be seen.

Let me say here that it is a daunting task to describe even the concept of time and space in the city of Heaven. How can I describe the dimensions of space when there is no limit to it? Both time and space were mostly focused on the present moment in front of me. Though I was aware of the immensity of Heaven's city, there was an intensity for experiencing the *now-ness* of God in both time and space. I will have to leave any further explanations to the theologians and scholars. I can only offer what I experienced and describe it in meager earthly words.

Many buildings were visible to me. Some had stately columns and grand arches as we might see on the Parthenon in Greece. But these structures were not made of hewn stone as on earth. The building material emanated a soft glow, unlike hard, cold materials such as marble or stone. These buildings exuded the love and warmth of God. I felt welcomed there.

> Both time and space were mostly focused on the present moment in front of me. Though I was aware of the immensity of Heaven's city, there was an intensity for experiencing the *now-ness* of God in both time and space.

The angel with me led me on a tour of some of the aspects of the city, answering the questions that came to my mind before I could even formulate them. I took notice of specific buildings as we encountered them. The buildings were used for different purposes. Among them were halls of great knowledge, halls of learning, halls of healing, and halls for music where all kinds of music could be heard—from what we would hear as classical, to very modern, to indescribable. This flow of music melded effortlessly with every sound in Heaven to become a melody reflecting the love of God, all flowing to a brilliant light that appeared to be the throne of God. As the golden streets grew nearer to the throne, their color became more transparent as some kind of crystal.

Halls of Knowledge

We came upon a beautiful building made of the same shimmering material as the others. I asked the angel, "What is this magnificent building?"

He replied, *"James, this is the hall of knowledge. It is the repository of all the prayers and petitions that mankind sends to Heaven and the throne of God."* I was reassured that nothing is ever lost to God. So the knowledge spoken of is God's knowledge of the heart of man and his deepest longings, which are cataloged there. Along with prayers, there were accounts of the deeds of people both good and evil. Again, nothing is lost to God. The halls of knowledge are where the books of each of our lives are kept.

Halls of Learning

As we continued on our way, the angel pointed out another building, which he referred to as halls of learning. Some of those who arrive in Heaven may be content to just enjoy the welcoming hospitality and wonders of Heaven. There are others who, throughout their earthly lives, found great joy in learning. These souls may wish to continue to grow and learn. There are libraries of amazing dimensions filled with knowledge from the beginnings of creation. The halls of learning also hold volumes of everything ever written about God and Jesus where these learners can go deeper into the incalculable mysteries of God.

Halls of Healing

To my surprise there were also halls of healing. This was not for physical healing, as all physical illness and pain are banished from Heaven.

These halls are for the healing of souls that led a painful life and who may have accepted Jesus even in their last moments. Some souls were so traumatized from a really difficult time on earth that they needed a period of adjustment in Heaven, and they were cared for in the halls of healing. They may have been caught up in drugs or trauma of every kind. Many, like me, cried out to God in their last moments of life on earth. God is so kind and gracious. In Heaven, "He will wipe every tear from their eyes, and there will be no more death or sorrow or crying or pain. All these things are gone forever."[2]

Dwelling Places in Heaven

I have been asked many times since sharing my vision of Heaven, "Did you see mansions for people in Heaven?" The answer is that all of Heaven is a dwelling place. There are houses of a sort that flowed with the entire landscape of Heaven. The houses appeared to be made with beautiful pastel colors having no sharp edges of any kind. They were rounded in an adobe kind of style and all flowed together into the landscape. (Some young folks have asked me if they were like "hobbit houses.")

Houses didn't appear to be a major factor in the city of Heaven. There are no rainy days in the city of Heaven—no weather, no storms or other things from which humans take shelter on earth. We don't need shelters or mansions. We are beings of light and spirit in Heaven, yet we have a definite form. While in Heaven I was not bound by any kind of physical body as on earth. There are, however, quiet places where we can go to be with our loved ones or to meditate on the love and mysteries of God. But there is nothing from which we need to take shelter.

---

2 Revelation 21:4, NLT

The Citizens of Heaven

While on my guided tour of Heaven I saw many, many people. The citizens of Heaven are beings of light reflecting the appearance of all nationalities and races—people of every tongue and tribe. Some were walking arm in arm while others gathered in family groups of their earthly loved ones. The faces of the people were filled with the love and life of Heaven. Each person I saw seemed to have a sense of purpose. This was not the look of trudging off to work for a paycheck; it was a look of joy and a sweet anticipation of delight, like a child on Christmas morning. Some carried books, others musical instruments of all kinds. Their purpose was just to be who they were with no burden or pretense. Everything they were to do in Heaven served as an act of worship to Christ. All of them were clothed in garments of shimmering light and all were infused with a sense of restful purpose.

> The citizens of Heaven are beings of light reflecting the appearance of all nationalities and races—people of every tongue and tribe.

There was something in their appearance that puzzled me. I turned to the angel and asked, "Are they all about the same age?" I would have guessed early 30s.

The angel responded with a beautiful and astounding answer. He said, *"Yes, James, God so loved Jesus and His sacrifice for mankind that He decreed that no one in Heaven would be any older than the age Jesus was when He died."* So, everyone in Heaven will appear to be in their early thirties. Some might wonder how we could identify a 95-year-old uncle or grandparent who passed on before us. Somehow, in the spirit, you will recognize them and they you. In Heaven, we are recognized more soul to soul than on the basis of age or appearance.

There were some exceptions. There were a few who appeared to be older and more distinguished. The angel explained that these were some of the prophets and patriarchs of the Bible. The other people stepped back in deference as they walked by. Their robes of light had a pastel quality to them. Another notable exception to those who appeared to be in their early thirties were children. And there were children playing everywhere! There were some who were very young, even infants.

The Nursery

We approached another building that held features different from the previous ones we had seen. The building before us was illuminated with alternating waves of soft light that shimmered across its surface from pink to blue and back to pink again. I asked, "What is this building?"

The angel replied, *"This is the nursery."*

"Nursery?" I said, astonished.

"Yes."

"How and why would there be a nursery in Heaven?" I asked.

The angel said, *"This is the nursery for souls of aborted babies or other babies miscarried or lost in their innocence."* He went on to tell me that the light of God was in each of these babies and that light longs to return to the Source—God Himself. They are cared for and raised to full age here in the love of God. Eventually they are free to join the general populace of Heaven.

I asked, "Are they like children of earth?"

The angel smiled and laughed, responding, *"They are very **much** like children on earth. And Jesus loves these children."*

> The angel said, "This is the nursery for souls of aborted babies or other babies miscarried or lost in their innocence."

I was told that this is where the souls of aborted children go until they can enter the fullness of their purpose in Heaven. They mature as on earth but much faster as they are beings of light. It's not about physical development; it's about growing in their purpose in Heaven. Again, it is difficult to understand or explain the passing of time or maturity within a timeless Heaven. But a two-year-old is like a six-year-old on earth. Some of those who come to maturity choose to stay on there to help other little souls on their journey to maturity in Heaven. God in His love and infinite mercy has a place for these little souls. Imagine the joy of a mother or father who finally enters Heaven only to find the little child they lost walking toward them, fully grown, with arms outstretched to welcome them in a heavenly embrace.

Furry Inhabitants of the City of Heaven

With all the wonders of Heaven that I have shared with people since my experiences there, I have to say that one of the most common questions I get regarding the city of Heaven is not about the buildings or people. People invariably ask, "Will I see my pet in Heaven?" We humans share life and affection with our pets. In truth, I saw dogs and cats and other animals all over the place, not to mention the beautiful horses. There is not a separate place for them. If you have something that you loved dearly in life and it returned that love to you, it will greet you in Heaven. No, they are not human, but somehow they represent love to us. I will leave it to the theologians once again to sort out the theology. I can report only what I experienced. I don't know what God's going to say to me when I show up with 11 horses that I've loved so dearly in my lifetime. Remember, any creature that had the

> If you have something that you loved dearly in life and it returned that love to you, it will greet you in Heaven.

capacity to bring joy and return love to you in some fashion will greet you in Heaven.

Heaven in its landscape, its design, and its residence is beautiful. It is a huge park and city stretching out in immense dimensions toward eternity. The atmosphere is one of love and joy. But for me, in my experience of Heaven, the greatest joy awaited me as I would stand face to face with Jesus.

Take the Journey

That you, being rooted and grounded in love, may be able to comprehend with all the saints what is the breadth and length and height and depth, and to know the love of Christ which surpasses knowledge, that you may be filled up to all the fullness of God.[3]

Theologians have tried for millennia to describe the love of God and the glories of Heaven. The entire Bible is the library of books whose sole purpose is to help us understand God's heart and plan for people. In the description of Heaven, love was seen in every direction and dimension. In the Scripture above, the apostle Paul desired that we would be able to experience the full dimension of the love of Christ. As you reflect on the images and dimensions of Heaven described in this chapter, allow yourself to be drawn beyond your understanding and see the love of God for what it really is—eternal in the heavens. It is broader, longer, higher, and deeper than we can describe in earthly terms. The only way to describe the love of God here is to experience it by faith knowing that it is beyond all we can ask or think or imagine. Yet it surrounds you even at this moment as you read these words. Let the love of God fill the landscape of your life.

Further Reflection

Here are a few things you might reflect upon concerning the love of God. Just as the angel provided the virtual tour of the dimensions of the city of Heaven, allow the Spirit of God to show you the dimensions of His love for you. The apostle Paul was very detailed in his description of the love of God for us. Take some time to reflect on his description

---

3 Ephesians 3:17-19

wherein he used terms we might otherwise use to describe the dimensions of a building. The love of God has breadth, length, height, and depth.

- **The broadness of God's love.** Take a few moments to allow the love of God to fill every part of your life— from your work, to your family and friends, to even the mundane acts of everyday living. His love is broad, filling every part of life. Ask the Holy Spirit to reveal any area of your life that needs to be bathed in the love of God.

- **The length of God's love.** Reflect now on the reality that God has loved you every day of your life, even in the places of pain or regret. Allow the love of God to fill your memories from your childhood to the present moment. His love is long, covering our lives from beginning to end. Sometimes it is helpful to look at our lives in segments along a timeline. To reflect on your life, use this simple timeline below marked in years of your lifetime. Think about the ways you either experienced the love of God in those years or, if you did not experience it, cover those years by acknowledging the love of God there.

| 0 | 10 | 20 | 30 | 40 | 50 | 60 | 70 | 80 |

- **The love of God is higher.** God's love is a spiritual love—a love beyond our ability to perform or return in the same measure it was given to us from God. Sit in awareness of your heart for a few moments, allowing yourself to simply receive the love of God based on His grace through the finished work on the cross of Jesus Christ. Where do you try to earn or repay the love of God? Where do you need to either receive grace or extend grace to other people, not based upon your performance or theirs but simply on God's grace and desire to love you?

- **The love of God is deeper.** The love of God desires to soak deeply into us to permeate every thought and motivation of our hearts. Be intentional about remembering the love of God that surrounds and soaks deeply into your life at every moment. The love of God is deeper in you than you can imagine. The Scriptures tell us that "deep calls to deep."[4] The deep love of God wants to soak into every part, every area, every word you speak, every motivation of your heart, and every moment of your life.

May the words that come out of my mouth and the musings of my heart meet with your gracious approval, O Eternal, my Rock, O Eternal, my Redeemer.[5]

Prayer

Gracious God, thank You for loving me with a broad love, a long love, a high love, and a deep love. I ask Your grace to cover every aspect of my life and to heal any area or time in my life when I was not aware of Your love. I give all of those times and places to You. Let me walk in the reality of that love at every moment by Your grace. Amen.

---

4 Psalm 42:7
5 Psalm 19:14, VOICE

Notes

CHAPTER EIGHT

Face to Face with Jesus

*Thus the Lord used to speak to Moses face to
face, just as a man speaks to his friend.*[1]

I was engrossed in the majesty and sheer dimension of all that I had
seen, so much that I lost track of the tallest angel who had been leading
me through Heaven. I was in awe of the flowers and was again aware of
the breeze and the gentle sound of Heaven's musical accompaniment all
around me that flowed to the very throne of God. As I turned around,
I noticed the tallest guardian a short distance away behind me on a little rise. I turned toward him and saw him bowing in reverence toward
a figure that was even taller than him. I wondered whether this was yet
another angel. But as brilliant as the other angel's robes were, this figure's
garment was as brilliant as the sun. His bearing was noble, and a golden

---

1 Exodus 33:11

light emanated from this figure making the light of the other angels seem dim by comparison. *Son-light.*

In awe, I turned right around and staggered slowly up the path toward the figure. This golden light flowed up and out of the figure like a fountain, cascading downward and pooling around Him. The golden flow encompassed everything around the figure. Even when the light would converge with the flowers around the figure, though they were already in bloom they bloomed even higher and more beautifully. The flowers stretched upward toward Him. This golden Son-light flowed from Him with the properties of liquid. I watched in fascination and awe as this light slowly made its way down the sloped path toward me. As it pooled around my feet, I was suddenly filled with the knowledge that this incredible figure was none other than Jesus Christ, the Son of the Living God. I had to get closer.

I had only taken a few steps when I was aware that the angels had come behind me and gently but firmly held me back.

The face of this figure was hidden from me at first. But there was a wavy shimmer surrounding Him like one might see on the surface of a road on a hot summer's day. His face was in profile to me. Though I could not see His face, there was a deep, soul-stirring perception that connected me to Him almost immediately. Then, when the flow of this light and love touched me, my spirit leapt with the realization that I was in the presence of the Lord of Heaven and earth—Jesus Christ! The light around me was *Son-light!*

> Though I could not see His face, there was a deep, soul-stirring perception that connected me to Him almost immediately. Then, when the flow of this light and love touched me, my spirit leapt with the realization that I was in the presence of the Lord of Heaven and earth—Jesus Christ! The light around me was Son-light!

Words are inadequate again to describe the appearance and bearing of the only begotten Son of God. He was not a picture in a children's Bible nor a legendary character. I was speechless at His appearance, though I could not yet see His face. He wore a simple yet beautiful seamless white garment with a red sash. There appeared to be no hem to this brilliant garment but a kind of golden mist that flowed at its base. The angels then bowed slightly and backed away in reverence to Jesus and went down on one knee. All became quiet before the King of Kings and Lord of Lords!

Suddenly, the shimmer vanished from the face of Jesus and He turned fully toward me. The angels who had been escorting me were beautiful, but now the face of Jesus was before me.

Seeing His face was the apex of my journey to Heaven. And what a face! This face was ruggedly handsome yet surprisingly human. His hair wasn't long like I would have expected from seeing many paintings and pictures depicting Jesus. His hair was brown and curled just over the collar of his robe.

Now, as I stood before Jesus, He smiled at me. The most radiant, beautiful, loving smile, like a father or a mother would give a son or a daughter. It was just overwhelmingly beautiful, and I felt the warmth of His smile flowing through me. His smile portrayed an unconditional love for me, someone who had never, ever acknowledged Him, who had turned away from Him at every turn along the way of my earthly life.

Then I saw the most striking and unforgettable aspect of Jesus' face—His eyes. The eyes of Jesus flashed with blue and gold and green drawing me into a deep sense of eternity. The eyes of Jesus were filled with relentless love for me—for you. These eyes that had never seen my devotion

> Then I saw the most striking and unforgettable aspect of Jesus' face—His eyes. The eyes of Jesus flashed with blue and gold and green drawing me into a deep sense of eternity.

or worship, that had never met my eyes looking for Him. His eyes spoke volumes to me, and as I gazed more deeply I saw something that moved me then and moves me to tears even now years later.

In those eyes was a well of both compassion and sorrow. There was sorrow for those who had not acknowledged or recognized Him. There was sadness for how I had personally lived my life apart from Him—so much time and life lost and squandered. Yet, there was a great love for me that so encompassed me that I felt as though I was the only person ever born. In those moments suspended in eternity, I was His sole focus. This same love is available for all people who know and turn toward Him. And with this gracious love flows forgiveness for all.

Now the tall angel stood in front of Jesus, and as he bowed low he brought something out from the sleeve of his robe. It appeared to be a very thin book of some kind, which the angel then opened for Jesus to read. It was as thin as a menu from a local diner. I don't know how, but somehow I knew that this was the book of my life filled with both good and bad. It was a thin volume with sparse entries of any kindness or love I had shown for my fellow man. My heart sank and my soul was crushed with the most incredible shame. I had invested my life in myself, mostly ignorant of the needs of other people around me. As Jesus began to read, the angel turned his face toward me, focusing those beautiful violet eyes on me. Then I heard his voice in my thoughts saying to me, "James, what did you do with the life my Master gave you?" Sadly, I had no answer.

I stood face to face with Jesus, exposed. I was filled with a deep despair and wondering how such indifference could dwell in the presence of such love. Yet, Jesus never referred to the thinness of that book. He never looked down on me with shame or judged me. The shame and regret were mine, not His. I had judged and condemned myself.

In the midst of this face-to-face encounter another feeling flowed from Jesus—joy! His face was set on the edge of a smile, and I knew that

His heart was to impart His joy to me. His joy had nothing to do with the volume of good things I had done whether thick or thin. As Jesus was silently reading the book, my life unfolded before me. The words He read became images that leapt off the pages of the book and into my mind—pictures of events from early childhood to the most recent days before my experience in Heaven. As they say, my life flashed before my eyes.

It didn't take Jesus long to read the thin book of my life. He had been inclined forward and now He straightened up with the angel now bowing more deeply. Though Jesus' stature didn't increase, He seemed to be even taller to me. The book was now closed and the angel replaced the book in the sleeve of his robe...and vanished.

I was filled with anticipation as it seemed that Jesus was about to speak to me. It is that feeling in the air before a thunderstorm that comes during a hot summer's day just before a clap of thunder. Then, I heard the most elegant, deep baritone voice speaking my name: *"James."* He spoke audibly to me now—not as thoughts transferred.

To hear that voice speaking my name penetrated to the deepest part of me. Jesus, the Son of God, spoke my name. His voice caused me to stagger for a moment, and I wanted to kneel as the angels had when Jesus first appeared but the angels kept me upright. When Jesus spoke my name, He held out His hand to me with the palm turned upward and toward me in a gesture of invitation. I tried to move forward and could not. I was frozen in awe. But when Jesus held out His hand, I saw the radiant light of His garment shining through a hole in His wrist—the wrist that had been nailed to the cross for me. For all of us. It was not a bloody or jagged hole, but clearly an odd-shaped scar He willingly took upon himself. The moment I realized it was the scar of the crucifixion I was filled with an

> But when Jesus held out his hand, I saw the radiant light of His garment shining through a hole in His wrist—the wrist that had been nailed to the cross for me.

overwhelming sense of profound sadness, guilt, and shame. I felt sadness for the savage way my sin had killed Him. I felt guilt for ignoring His sacrifice all my life. I felt shame for the life I had led. It was so personal and intense a moment it was as though I had held the hammer and driven the nails into His body.

Now Jesus looked directly at me with eyes filled with compassion and love. Something life changing happened in that brief encounter. How I long to see those eyes again. All that I had searched for my entire life was fulfilled in those eyes and the words He spoke to me.

He Knows My Name

Now Jesus fixed His total attention on me and spoke: *"James...my son...this is not yet your time. Go back...and tell your brothers and sisters...of the wonders we have shown you."* While these words were brief, they were long on meaning for me. Though Jesus didn't speak many words to me, they were powerful and transformational.

"James." To hear the God who created everything speak my name had deep meaning for me. He knew my name. I was not some anonymous blob of humanity. I had a name and He was speaking it! As Jesus spoke my name, I sensed my value in His eyes. Jesus knows who I am. When Jesus spoke my name, it was as though I was the only person ever born. His next words poured life into my empty heart and fulfilled a longing I'm just now understanding.

> "James, my son, this is not yet your time. Go back and tell your brothers and sisters of the wonders we have shown you."

"My son." I had longed to know a father—a dad. From my school days when I would occasionally climb the hill to the cemetery where my earthly father was buried, I wanted a dad. Many times, I longed to hear my father answer the frequent questions that all kids have. Though I had a great

father figure in my grandfather, all kids notice the absence of a dad. Dads teach a kid how to throw a ball or steady them as they learn to ride a bicycle. Being called *son* also made me a part of the family of God and gave me a new identity and purpose beyond myself.

"This is not yet your time." This meant to me that there *would be* a time when I would find Heaven again as my home for eternity…to live in the "now-ness" of God forever. Forever present. Forever known. How I yearn and long for that time when I will see Jesus face to face again, living in the city of the King for eternity. But His next words moved me from joy to sorrow.

"Go back and tell your brothers and sisters of the wonders we have shown you." His words were not a suggestion; they were a mission and I was His agent. I must come back to my question—who am I? Who am I to tell anybody anything about God and Heaven? I am not a preacher or Bible scholar. In fact, I've not spoken before crowds of Christian people or churches. In the world's estimation, I was not a bad person, but I might take ethics to the edge in a business deal. Life was all about me. Now, having received this commission from the mouth of Jesus, my arrogance was revealed. Before my experience with Heaven and Jesus Christ, I was only concerned about what I possessed. Now my life was possessed by Him. My qualification for this new mission would have to come from the sheer grace of God. I was out of control.

> How could it be that I was being sent away? I had finally come home.

The experiences and the heart of Heaven had begun a process of transformation and compassion in me. Though I can tell this great story, the greatest evidence of its truthfulness is my own transformation. I carry Heaven in my heart with me into all of life. As I look into the eyes of other folks, I cannot help but recall the eyes of Jesus as we stood face to face.

The Assignment

Now, staggering somewhere between fear and joy, I tried to move toward Him but the angels held me back. I had interpreted Jesus' reaching out toward me as an invitation. But the hand that was extended toward me to reveal the scars of His passion now rotated upward with His palm toward me. My heart stopped.

My heart was grieved. How could it be that I was being sent away? I had finally come home; my yearning was being fulfilled in that moment. I began to tearfully plead with Jesus, "Lord, please let me stay. I won't be any trouble. Jesus let me stay with You."

The angels were now holding me back, and I remember trying to struggle past them to get to Jesus. It was pretty useless to resist angels that were more than twice or three times my size. To my astonishment, when I turned once again to plead with Jesus, He was no longer there. In His place stood the tallest angel who had suddenly reappeared. He looked at me with tender loving-kindness and with some sorrow said, *"I'm sorry, James, but you have to go."* As he spoke, he extended his wings, clothed in immense power and authority, but barring my way forward.

The next thing I knew, I was in the same tunnel that transported me to Heaven traveling in that same silent, windless light speed. And then I was aware of a different face and a far less gentle voice raised toward me: "James! James!"

Take the Journey

Thus the Lord used to speak to Moses face to face, just as a man speaks to his friend.[2]

Think, for a moment, of the Lord of Heaven and earth holding the book of your life filled with the acts and attitudes of your life on earth. What would He see in that book? Then, understand that His joy is not dependent on the contents of your book whether thick or thin. True, each man's works will be revealed,[3] but the joy of the Lord comes from His character. He *is* joy! "For the joy set before Him [Jesus] endured the cross."[4]

As you reflect on this chapter, think about the joy the Lord has *in* you; not what you've done or accomplished: you! Focus on that joy. His joy is standing face to face with you. When He was being nailed to the cross He was thinking of you. You were the joy set before Christ. Breathe in the joy of the Lord as you stand in His presence. Let your joy be full in Jesus Christ. Live from now on as though you have nothing to lose.

Further Reflection

Between Abba and us there is the tangled junk of performance and the many ways we've tried to earn what was already freely ours. Likewise, the Father's passion to see our faces is obstructed with sin, self-effort, and issues growing from the bitter roots of past hurts. This junk cannot be overlooked

---

2 Exodus 33:11
3 1 Corinthians 3:13
4 Hebrews 12:2

and shoved aside; it must be hauled out to the curb with the rest of the trash.[5]

Envision the time when you stand face to face with Jesus. Now imagine that the Lord is speaking the words of the Scripture above directly to you. What do you hear Him saying? What is the tone of His voice to you? Do you hear a scolding tone? Or is His voice more invitational? Do you find yourself trying to impress Jesus with the works you've done? The Scriptures tell us that the things we do *for* Jesus are like dirty laundry.

> *We are all infected and impure with sin. When we display our righteous deeds, they are nothing but filthy rags. Like autumn leaves, we wither and fall, and our sins sweep us away like the wind.*[6]

It is the joy of Christ that we can stand face to face with Him as Adam walked in precious fellowship with Him in the cool of the day. Rather than do works *for* Jesus, let's think of doing them *with* Him. Listen again to the tone and words of His voice. You may want to look at Psalm 19:7-10 to see the character of the voice of God. I have condensed it here for you.

The Sound of God's Voice

When I hear God speaking to me, His voice is:

- Healing—inviting me to God Himself.
- Clear—allowing me to respond.
- Right—giving me joy.
- Pure—enlightening me about myself.
- Enduring—true, righteous, clean, giving me confidence.

---

5 Gardner, *Living the God-Breathed Life*, 84.
6 Isaiah 64:6, NLT

- Desirable—sweet, drawing me close, resulting in worship.[7]

When God is speaking to us He draws us to Himself. It is His greatest joy and desire that we would know and walk with Him forever!

Prayer

*Gracious Lord, I desire to stand face to face with You—to live in Your presence moment by moment. As I am face to face with You I ask that all false notions I have of You would be healed. I also give You all the things I've done **for** You to try and earn the favor that is freely mine by Your grace and sacrifice on the cross alone. I thank You for knowing my name. Amen.*

---

7 Gardner, *Healing the Wounded* Heart, 65.

Notes

CHAPTER NINE

The Return Journey

*I know a man in Christ who fourteen years ago—whether
in the body I do not know, or out of the body I do not
know, God knows—such a man was caught up to the third
heaven. And I know how such a man—whether in the
body or apart from the body I do not know, God knows—
was caught up into Paradise and heard inexpressible
words, which a man is not permitted to speak.*[1]

Back in the Tunnel

With the angel's voice still resonating in my heart, I was drawn back
into the same tunnel that carried me to the fields of Heaven, and it felt as
though I was traveling even faster than before. I could see the light at the

---

1 2 Corinthians 12:2-4

end of the tunnel, though this was a dimmer, earthly light. This would not be as soft a landing as my journey to Heaven. I was sliding down through the tunnel and beginning to feel something I had almost forgotten while in Heaven—pain. In those moments, there was no thought of the mission to tell my brothers and sisters anything—only the reintroduction to my earthly life.

Now the euphoria of Heaven, angels, and the face of Jesus was being replaced with the descent into my physical body and pain. I felt something strange on my face—a slapping that grew in intensity with each blow. I was told later that the doctor was trying to revive me by slapping my face. It was as if I was being delivered the way you would stimulate a newborn child. Maybe that's what a newborn baby experiences going from the security of the womb into this cold world. It was as if I was being truly born again.

> The world and my physical body felt like a cold, wet, slimy place to live. I began to feel an overwhelming sense of the loss of Heaven.

The world and my physical body felt like a cold, wet, slimy place to live. I began to feel an overwhelming sense of the loss of Heaven. Gradually, I could feel the oxygen mask, meant to bring air, actually seeming to obstruct it. My body was covered by a white sheet. With each breath and beat of my heart the precincts of Heaven grew more faint. I was suffocating in my earthly body. At the same time the boundless freedom of Heaven was being supplanted by a strange feeling of captivity.

The full reality of what had happened was beginning to dawn on me. I was connected to a respirator, and when I began to breathe on my own the alarm began to go off. To everyone's shock I was alive! How could this be? I was gone and now was back again. Apparently, they wrote, "Eleven hours with no sign of brain activity." Nonetheless, here I was, alive!

It is impossible to describe the contrast between where I found myself and where I had been only moments earlier. The music of Heaven's flowers was replaced by frantic sounds of medical activity. The warmth of Heaven's home was now supplanted by a cold and hostile place. The soothing voices of the angels were now sounds of medical terms concerning me, and the calm of Heaven's garden was now a personal maze of confusion. What was happening to me?

My first lucid thought was, *Where is Lorraine?* The hospital called my wife from the quiet room and explained to her what had happened to everyone's medical amazement. (You will hear this from Lorraine's perspective in the following chapter.) Lorraine came rushing in. I tried to speak to her but my voice and air were obstructed, as I had been intubated because I was not able to breathe on my own.

I was back but in terrible shape. My physical body was seriously ill. At least one of my lungs had collapsed, and I had a raging case of pneumonia. I spent a long time in the ICU. I had tubes down my throat and I couldn't speak to tell anyone of my experience. As I regained consciousness the tubes were removed. I grabbed Lorraine's hand and said, "Lorraine, I was in Heaven...I saw Jesus...Jesus had horses!"

> I grabbed Lorraine's hand and said, "Lorraine, I was in Heaven...I saw Jesus...Jesus had horses!"

Lorraine said, "I don't know what you saw, but you've been going on about seeing Jesus." She said, "I know you better than anyone. I couldn't make out what you were saying." The tubes really ruptured my vocal chords. But as soon as I could speak to any degree, I kept telling this story to her. I seemed desperate to report what I had seen.

Putting the Story Together

An amazing part of my experience were the doctors who were surprised at my return and recovery. I am forever grateful for the professional and compassionate care I received while in the hospital. From the doctors to the other medical staff, the care was first rate. At first, my prospects for recovery or even life itself were dim. For all intents and purposes I was gone. I had no brain activity for several hours.

At first when I awakened, the story of my experience was as disconnected as I was connected to medical devices. I have the analytical mind of a pilot and businessman, and I'm always trying to figure things out—to get my position right. Some aspects—the angels, the flowers, and mostly the eyes of Jesus—were intact, if out of sequence. The amount of time was a mystery to me. Others with similar experiences have reported events that took hours when in fact they were gone for only minutes. I don't think time is very important in Heaven and the realm of the Spirit. We live our life by the clock as creatures of linear time. In Heaven, past, present, and future collapse into an eternal now. No one is looking at their watch there. Eventually, I began to put the timelines and sequence of the experience together.

Pastor Luke Weaver, Jr., leads a church 50 minutes from us. Our daughters have done rodeo together. Before my experience, I knew him casually but paid little attention to his spiritual activities or position. He was "one of those Christians" and a pastor. I didn't want anything to do with that. Pastor Luke had come to the hospital earlier to pray with Lorraine and ask if there was anything he could do.

The more time passed from my experience, the more I began to try and make sense of it. I had been questioning myself as to the reality of all I saw. Was it drug-induced? Was it a hallucination? When Pastor Luke visited me I began to tell him of the doctor's report to me, that the medical staff had done nothing that would have induced that hallucination. In fact, there was no brain activity. Luke then told me the most important thing I had heard since my experience in Heaven: "Jim, I believe you." This gave me the courage to continue to share my experience.

Once I was well enough, I sat down at Pastor Luke's huge kitchen table and said, "Luke, I'm really worried that there is something wrong with me."

"What's bothering you?" Luke inquired.

I responded, "Luke, I wake up somewhere around 3:00 A.M. out of my sleep recalling and almost reliving my experience in Heaven. I begin to write furiously. Then I get up in the morning and read what I've written. I've filled more than five journals. There is so much and it is so vivid. Luke, did I dream all of this? Is this my imagination? It has been such a psychological journey for me."

> Did I dream all of this? Is this my imagination?

I read some of my journaling to Luke with his wife Bonnie sitting nearby. As happens many times, the wisdom began to flow from her. She said, "Jim, look, the experience that you had was so overwhelming, so all-encompassing of your senses, that if God had intended you to know all of that at once, you couldn't have stood it. You couldn't have taken it. You would have blown your mind." And she was right. It was like many folks who have a shocking experience that takes time to unfold and understand.

No, I have not become the sage who came from Heaven. There are many things I saw and heard in Heaven that I do not yet understand. I try to share my experience the best I can. Some that I do not understand I will likely never share. There are eternal truths that I still try to understand with an earth-bound mind. While in Heaven, it was as though information was being downloaded into my soul. However, I do not have all the answers to all of the questions people have asked me about Heaven. I still wrestle with the question, "Who am I?" (that God should allow me to experience all of these wonders of Heaven).

As our times together unfolded, Pastor Luke would sit at the table with me while I shared the emerging details of what I could remember. As I said previously, I had begun to recall and record the details of all I experienced in Heaven in several volumes of a personal journal. I had little or no biblical knowledge, but as details of the experience arose, Pastor Luke referred me to Scripture. For example, when I mentioned about there being no sun or celestial source of light in Heaven, Pastor Luke referred me to the book of Revelation. "And the city has no need of the sun or of the moon to shine on it, for the glory of God has illumined it, and its lamp is the Lamb."[2] Each part of my experience began to be clarified with Luke's guidance. He became a mentor to me as did his wonderful and godly extended family of Grace Chapel in Pennsylvania. I will be forever grateful for Luke's patient heart as he listened to me and the Holy Spirit at the same time, beginning to make sense of what I learned in Heaven. Most of what I learned was about the heart of Jesus and my relationship with Him.

> I had the most extravagant experience, then had to come back and learn about what I had experienced. The example came before the lesson.

I realize that my process in putting all of my story together was the reverse of how most folks learn. Most of the time we would read and study a matter, then have some experience or object lesson to reinforce what we have learned. But in this case, I had the most extravagant experience, then had to come back and learn about what I had experienced. The example came before the lesson. It was like being sent to a foreign land where I didn't know the language but learned more as I was immersed in that country and culture.

The thing that remains with me is the longing for the presence of Jesus. Yet even in this life on earth, for which I'm grateful, I have come to an assurance that there is more—that there is a longing on

---

2 Revelation 21:23

both sides of the veil to be reunited with Christ for eternity, to see those amazing eyes again and hear the resonant voice of Jesus speaking my name once more. I'm grateful for the life I have now and that I have been given a mission to tell you about all that I experienced. The yearning for Heaven persists and the knowledge that I was created to love and be loved by God.

There is no medical or practical explanation for what happened to me or even why it happened. But the fulfillment of my yearning is now as close as my memory of my experience of Heaven and Jesus. It is as close as speaking the name, Jesus. Jesus.

Take the Journey

*I know a man in Christ who fourteen years ago—whether
in the body I do not know, or out of the body I do not know,
God knows—such a man was caught up to the third heaven.
And I know how such a man—whether in the body or apart
from the body I do not know, God knows—was caught up
into Paradise and heard inexpressible words, which a man is
not permitted to speak.[3]*

We humans are always striving to understand and interpret our lives
in human terms. If life does not add up, then something must be amiss.
We might imagine the confusion of the first followers of Jesus on earth
who could not add it all up even though they had the greatest teacher
in history. Scripture tells us that Jesus came to His own people and they
missed Him completely.[4] How much more difficult is it for us to try to
interpret or understand the spiritual realities around us? The things of
the Spirit of God are spiritual and not always discernable to the understanding of man. Jesus breathed the Spirit and understanding into His
first followers. We should ask Him for the same breath.

Further Reflection

The most brilliant minds cannot fathom the mysteries of God. Listen
to the apostle Paul:

*For consider your calling, brethren, that there were not many
wise according to the flesh, not many mighty, not many noble;
but God has chosen the foolish things of the world to shame
the wise, and God has chosen the weak things of the world to*

---

3 2 Corinthians 12:2-4
4 John 1:11

shame the things which are strong, and the base things of the world and the despised God has chosen, the things that are not, so that He may nullify the things that are, so that no man may boast before God.[5]

Take time to lay down your desire to understand the mystery of God and simply experience God in the mystery. How should we do this? Simply close your eyes and speak the name that is above all names with me—Jesus. Jesus. Let yourself see His face and hear His voice. Allow the deep longing in your heart to connect with His heart. Jesus says, "Behold, I stand at the door and knock; if anyone hears My voice and opens the door, I will come in to him and will dine with him, and he with Me."[6]

Prayer

Gracious Lord Jesus, I thank You for every step of my spiritual journey, even those where I've stumbled and turned off the pathway. I am in awe of Your generous grace that calls me back to You and the way You continue to reveal Yourself to me. I desire to live close to You every moment. Amen.

---

5 1 Corinthians 1:26-29
6 Revelation 3:20

Notes

CHAPTER TEN

The View from This Side of Heaven

LORRAINE'S STORY

*Now to Him who is able to do far more abundantly beyond
all that we ask or think, according to the power that
works within us, to Him be the glory in the church and in
Christ Jesus to all generations forever and ever. Amen.*[1]

My sleep was restless. I was very tired from working extra hours at the long-term care nursing home where I serve. Jim said he might go to the movies and had not yet come home. I had woken up several times through

---

1 Ephesians 3:20-21

the night. Something was wrong. At one point, I thought I heard some-one rattling around the kitchen and assumed it was Jim. Somewhere in the early morning, my workplace called and awakened me for good, but Jim was still not home. I got up and looked around the house and outside. Jim would usually be up tending to our horses in the early morning. But he was not there. His truck was not there. Where was he? I began to call Jim's cell phone repeatedly, but there was no answer.

I walked quickly from place to place; my heart began to fill with anxiety, my pulse was increasing, and my breath growing shallower with each step. Rolling around in the back of my mind was the prayer that I offered a short time earlier. Though Jim was not a deeply spiritual person then, he had at least gone to church occasionally. In recent years, however, he had grown more preoccupied with his business and his pain and had wandered even further away from anything to do with God or church. Years before, I had begun to pray, "Lord, if You must break Jim to remake him, do it." Now, my petition of recent years to break Jim filled me with guilt. Had something happened to him? Was this the doing of my prayer? Was this my fault? Where was Jim? I had a bad feeling that something was terribly wrong.

Entering into full alarm, I called my sister, Shelley, but spoke to her husband, David. He relayed to me that Shelley too had been awakened several times during the night to pray, though she didn't know for whom or what. But there was a sense of urgent intercession in her prayer. Out of the blue, another sister, Jean, was also awakened to urgent prayer. She felt God was telling her to call David and Shelley immediately. Jean thought her prayer burden might have been for our father, who was ill and in the same hospital Jim would eventually be taken to. I added a call for advice to a family friend, a firefighter, Gerry, who told me to call the Royal Canadian Mounted Police (RCMP).

The RCMP came to the house and talked to me and got the number to Jim's cell phone so that they could use it to find his location. Soon there was a small group at our home—three of my sisters, one of their sons, and a brother-in-law. Our friend the firefighter stood close by but was not with us in the prayer circle. There were six of us whose hands found each other in the middle of our kitchen as we joined in a circle to pray for Jim. None of us had any idea what had happened nor what Jim was experiencing at that moment in Heaven. While they were looking for Jim, Jean's son Matthew, Shelly, her husband David leading the prayer, another sister Karen, and I held hands and were praying that Jim would be found soon, alive, and kept safe. David led the prayer that if it was the will of Jesus, He would send Jim back to us. We had no idea what the RCMP would soon find.

As we were holding on to one another in prayer, a knock came to the door. It was a constable from the RCMP. He entered the house with a concerned look on his face. Removing his hat, he said, "We have located your husband Mrs. Woodford, and it doesn't look good. We were able to break into the truck where we found him. Paramedics are working on him and there is a faint heartbeat, but it doesn't look good. They are taking him to the trauma unit at the hospital." One thing that had complicated Jim's medical condition was that it was very cold and he had been in his truck without a coat.

With that, the constable took me to the trauma unit at the hospital. My sister Karen was with me. It was all surreal to me, as though I were living some kind of night terror. I was numb and in shock. When we arrived, the physician came in to the quiet room adjacent to the trauma unit to talk to me. The constable stayed by me while I talked to the physician. Neither the doctor nor I had any idea what had happened to Jim. The doctor

There were six of us whose hands found each other in the middle of our kitchen as we joined in a circle to pray for Jim. None of us had any idea what had happened nor what Jim was experiencing at that moment in Heaven.

asked me if Jim was on any kind of medication and I described what Jim had been taking. He stood by listening, trying to get an idea of what had happened. But there was nothing to be done for Jim now.

They transferred him out of the trauma unit to ICU. An attendant escorted me to a quiet room off the ICU. There a doctor spoke to me in a kind voice saying, "Mrs. Woodford, your husband has no brain sign. He is clinically deceased and has been intubated. We are keeping his breathing and heart going, but not for long. There is nothing we can do for Jim. You will have to let him go. If you have anyone who wants to see Jim before he is disconnected then please ask them to come immediately." By this time, Jim's kidneys and the rest of his body had begun to shut down. As an RN, I knew what these signs meant—there was no hope.

> After hours of no brain activity, Jim's eyes suddenly opened! His various systems began to function once again! We were all astonished!

I updated my sisters regarding Jim's condition and the doctor's report. All the while my sisters at home, Shelly and Jean, continued to pray that Jim would be fully restored. They are relentless and faithful prayer warriors.

Now they took me into the room to see Jim. Though I had been an RN for years, I was taken aback by the sight of Jim hooked up to several machines. This was a strange sight for me. Jim was always full of life, independent, confident. He was known as "Diamond Jim." It seemed he could do or fix anything or handle any problem. Even in the face of serious problems, Jim would say, "That's not a big deal; we can fix that." Now he lay motionless and still. His life signature had been reduced to the single beeping of the heart monitor. How many more beeps would there be until we heard that last, long signal and he would be gone? The words of my prayer kept coming back to disturb me: "Lord, if You must, break him to remake him."

I too prayed for Jim to be restored even though, as a nurse, I understood the words of the doctor. I prayed that God would restore Jim and that he would not be impaired in any way. All I could do now was to pray, all the while feeling the guilt from my prayer, "Break him to remake him." All at once, one of the ICU nurses came to me and said, "Mrs. Woodford, please come here quickly." Now there were medical people rushing around everywhere. After hours of no brain activity, Jim's eyes suddenly opened! His various systems began to function once again! We were all astonished!

I began to wonder how much of Jim could possibly still be there. He had been brain dead and much of his body shut down for many hours. Now, with his eyes opened, Jim was trying to talk to me but he had been intubated and couldn't speak. After a while, as his breathing slowly improved, they removed the respirator but kept it on standby. Jim was struggling to talk with a scratchy, gravelly voice, so I bent my head down to listen closely and to my astonishment I heard Jim say, "I saw Jesus, and Jesus has horses!" None of this made sense to me at the moment. I had no idea what Jim had seen or experienced. I was still wondering how much of him was there. I was just feeling thankful and knew I was seeing the power of God and that He had answered our prayers.

Jim seemed bewildered and was frantically looking around to get his bearings. He began to spill out what he had seen in Heaven. The wonderful medical crew was trying to keep Jim calm and quiet, but he was excited and insistent to tell all that happened. He had at least one collapsed lung and was filled with pneumonia. He was not going anywhere soon.

Meanwhile, my daughter, who is friends with Pastor Luke Weaver's daughters, had asked if they would stop by and pray for Jim. They were in town and only a few minutes from the hospital where Jim was. They were not totally aware of what had happened but were allowed to come in for a few minutes to pray for Jim. Jim does not clearly remember their visit. Little did any of us realize that God had a plan for Jim.

Jim was in the hospital for weeks on antibiotics and coughing up a tar-like substance from the pneumonia and collapsed lung. I helped him in the hospital as he was very sick. He had to move with a walker. Eventually Jim was discharged and came home. That was the beginning of another kind of season—a season of finding purpose in all that had happened to Jim and all he had seen and heard in Heaven.

Jim was once again very weak and in recovery. His business activity was mostly gone and things began to collapse around us financially. In the meantime, a friend drove up to our house, asking about Jim, "Lorraine, what are you going to do?" I must admit that at that moment I didn't know what we were going to do, but I knew that God was trustworthy and that He had a purpose for all that had happened. My constant encouragement to Jim was, "You were brought back for a purpose." How well would Jim be? We had to wait to see how he would recover.

> God had a purpose for Jim's experience and return, and He would put people where they needed to be to help with the mission he was assigned.

Jim was making a surprisingly good physical recovery, yet he was in confusion and depression saying, "Everything is gray here. I don't want to be here. You don't know what I've seen. What am I going to do? How do I tell people what I've seen?"

I just kept saying, "There is a reason you are back." Jim's only experience of public speaking had been in a few secular gatherings of entrepreneurs.

The Lord was gracious in the way He met our needs and expenses. I was able to pick up extra shifts, and we were able to sell off things that we no longer needed like boats and cars. Yet Jim was still depressed. I called home often from work to make sure he was okay. But Jim was in a place of transformation and readjustment to his earthly life. He would say things like, "If you could have seen what I saw...heard the flowers sing-ing...seen colors beyond the earth...it is hard to live in this gray place."

I came home many a day to find Jim sitting head in hands, despon-dent and depressed, not wanting anyone around. I would remind him that God sent him back to spread the word of what he had seen. He would respond, "I don't know anything about the Bible. I'm not a holy man or preacher."

Jim thought that he would be ridiculed or, worse, that he would be seen as prospering off his experience with Jesus in Heaven. My reply was always that God had a purpose for Jim's experience and return and that He would put people where they needed to be to help with the mission he was assigned. "He will show us," I said. My prayers began to shift toward the mission—*Lord, help Jim to respond to Your words and fill him with the Holy Spirit.* Prayers now shifted. *Respond, fill with the Spirit.*

> He stepped outside of himself and felt as though Someone else was speaking through him.

Soon, a couple of my coworkers began to ask Jim to come and speak of his experience. He would not go. Then, Jim was asked to speak at Pastor Luke's church. Again, he was reluctant, but he went and something momentous happened in that safe environment. The dam burst and Jim began to share freely. It was as through Jim felt safe enough to get out of the way and let God speak through him. He said he stepped outside of himself and felt as though Someone else was speaking through him. Jim was remembering the glories of Heaven and little by little, memories and tears erupted with newfound emotion. He had begun to fulfill the command Jesus had given to him, "James, My son, go and tell your brothers and sisters of the wonders we have shown you." He had found new purpose in his life.

From the very beginning of this journey, God answered our prayers even before we joined hands in our kitchen. I recognize that my prayer to break and remake Jim began in the heart of God. The fact that my sisters were called to prayer in the middle of the night was evidence of God's plan. Again, if my workplace had not called I would not have been awakened and noticed that Jim was not home that night he spent in the truck. God was working through it all.

I ask myself the same question Jim asks himself, "Lord, who am I?" All of this has had an amazing effect on Jim. He is becoming much gentler, more caring, patient, empathetic, kind, and tender toward me and other people. Not to mention that Jim has become a good cook. We joke that instead of becoming a vegetable he now cooks them!

> God has a plan and now we work together to pursue Him and His plan.

This experience has changed both of us. As a long-term care RN, I have served many who are in life's final hours and in transition toward eternity. I now find myself praying for them with even more compassion and bringing them peace. God is truly good. He has a plan. We can now see the hand of God in things such as Jim seeing our prayers for him as contrails in Heaven while we were standing in the prayer circle in our kitchen.

God has a plan and now we work together to pursue Him and His plan.

Take the Journey

Now to Him who is able to do far more abundantly beyond all that we ask or think, according to the power that works within us, to Him be the glory in the church and in Christ Jesus to all generations forever and ever. Amen.[2]

It is a good thing for us that God is not limited by our imaginations. Jesus prayed "on earth as it is in Heaven." Sometimes we are unaware that we are caught up in God's plan as Lorraine was when she began to pray, "Lord, break him to remake him." God's plan and power are at work in and around us. We must grow quieter to listen to the voice of the Spirit to become part of that plan.

There is power in agreement. When we join hands to pray it is as though we are opening a portal of communication with the heart of God. Lorraine and her family were praying in agreement with what God had already purposed to do.

Further Reflection

Read this short paragraph and allow yourself to become quiet to hear the voice of the Spirit. Meditate on the Scripture below and allow the Lord to speak to you personally through words, thoughts, images, or whatever other means He chooses.

Again, I say unto you, That if two of you shall agree on earth as touching any thing that they shall ask, it shall be done for them of my Father which is in heaven. For where two or three

---

2 Ephesians 3:20-21

are gathered together in my name, there am I in the midst of them.[3]

Prayer

Gracious Lord, I pray that my heart may be confident in Your love for me so that I might, through the Holy Spirit, be praying back to You what is in Your heart. May my prayer be a reflection of Your love and establish Your kingdom on the earth. Amen.

3 Matthew 18:19-20, KJV

Notes

CHAPTER ELEVEN

An Exchange of Yokes

Come to Me, all who are weary and heavy-laden,
and I will give you rest. Take My yoke upon you
and learn from Me, for I am gentle and humble
in heart, and you will find rest for your souls.
For My yoke is easy and My burden is light.[1]

I have now had a couple of years to process and understand my experience. There are still unanswered questions in my mind, like, *Why me?* I could just as well have passed away and fallen into the crevasse of Hell and eternal destruction I encountered at the other end of the tunnel of light. Those claws that reached out from the pit may have dragged me into the waiting jaws of darkness. But they didn't. Gratitude doesn't begin to describe my attitude toward God for saving me on such a thin request:

---

1 Matthew 11:28-30

"God forgive me—God help me." I will meditate on this question until I stand before Jesus again, this time with a one-way ticket and residential status in Heaven. (Dr. Thom will talk further about this thin request a little later.)

Much of what I want to share in this chapter has to do with what I learned about the heart of God Himself. The words directly spoken to me by Jesus in Heaven were few. But all of Heaven, from the angels even to the landscape of Heaven filled with light, all communicates something of the heart and love of God. Therefore, in this chapter I want to recount what was given to me about God Himself through all the various aspects I have previously described. All of these aspects are echoes of the heart of God. What does my experience in Heaven say about God and His Son Jesus Christ? How have these realities changed me and the way I see life following my experience in Heaven? The comments are not long, but they speak long about the heart of God. Thom will add a Scripture verse for reflection at the end of each of the truths I've learned. The instruction is simple—read and reflect on the Scriptures and how they might become part of your life as well.

God is:

A Constant Friend

First and foremost, a phrase that was spoken over and over by the angels in Heaven was that of "constant friend." God is a constant Friend, and friends share life together. Friends influence one another. Friends are there for one another. Through my experience in Heaven, I am now aware that there are no unimportant aspects of our lives. I know that God is close to me and, just for the asking, He will speak into any part of my life. God is constant, and He is a friend.

Read and Reflect

> *No longer do I call you slaves, for the slave does not know what his master is doing; but I have called you friends, for all things that I have heard from My Father I have made known to you.*[2]

A God of Heroic Grace and Forgiveness

God overflows with grace and forgiveness. God is the God who responds to us in our most dire circumstances—when the boat is sinking and going under the waves, God bails us out. God and His Son, Jesus, are eternal romantics. He is moving toward us even when we don't expect it. He responded to my call for help on the cusp of Hell on the thinnest request.

God was not intimidated by my lifelong apathy and inattention to His love for me. God is the God of second and third chances and more. Of course, my callous inattention had consequences for me and others around the landscape of my life. (Thom will elaborate more on this in the next chapter.) I did nothing to merit a glimpse of Heaven and the escape from Hell. These were all God's generous love and grace to me. But I do think of all the people I might have helped with the resources I had previously. I just

> God, who knew me better than I knew myself, allowed me to see the wonders of His heavenly kingdom.

didn't see God or the people around me in any meaningful way. Life was all about me. But God, who knew me better than I knew myself, allowed me to see the wonders of His heavenly kingdom, which I still struggle to take in or describe. He did this on the thinnest request for forgiveness. He has revealed His extravagant grace to me. By that same grace, I will reveal it to other folks.

---

2 John 15:15

Read and Reflect

Call upon Me in the day of trouble; I shall rescue you, and you will honor Me.[3]

God of Compassionate Hospitality

God meets us where we are and brings us to Himself with compassion. During my experience in Heaven, God made me feel "at home" by bringing me familiar things from the album of my life story like the thought of tapioca pudding and horses in Heaven's pastures. Heaven was presented as a warm and hospitable place. God knew the dimension of adjustment of the journey to Heaven and all of the medical challenges I dealt with that led up to my passing. God made me comfortable, much like we might put the favorite foods of dinner guests on the table. It is a humbling thought that the most powerful entity in the universe chose to make me feel at home. God knows us. He knew the paths that I walked in my life and made a way for me to Himself. God knew my life well.

> It is a humbling thought that the most powerful entity in the universe chose to make me feel at home.

God knew the longing in the heart of this fatherless child. God knew my futile attempts to fulfill the longing emptiness inside of me that I tried to fill with more things. He responded to my emptiness by filling me with wonder. God is a God of compassionate hospitality.

Read and Reflect

Blessed be the God and Father of our Lord Jesus Christ, the Father of mercies and God of all comfort, who comforts us in all our affliction so that we will be able to comfort those who

---

3 Psalm 50:15

are in any affliction with the comfort with which we ourselves are comforted by God.[4]

God of the Impossible

God has changed me inside and out. He has turned my life in a totally new direction. Nothing is impossible with God. I was faced with a health obstacle that limited and could have eventually taken my life. God is the God of the impossible. I cannot describe the contrast from the incredible and disabling pain and paralysis of my illness to the healing that I experienced in Heaven. Though the indications of the disease are still in my physical body, I have no symptoms of it. My recovery has baffled the doctors and blessed my family. But I was also living in an emotional pain and paralysis, which He is healing. When I returned back to life in my physical body, I had a period of recovery, but there were no symptoms of the disease in my body. My healing was the residue of Heaven sent back with me—an evidence of the love of God. The eternal God took a retired pilot and is transforming him into a messenger of God's love and grace. He is turning my focus to the people around me. He is transforming me into a living epistle to speak of His heart that is expressed in every aspect of Heaven. I am truly convinced that nothing is impossible with God.

Read and Reflect

> *For truly I say to you, if you have faith the size of a mustard seed, you will say to this mountain, "Move from here to there," and it will move; and nothing will be impossible to you.*[5]

---

4 2 Corinthians 1:3-4
5 Matthew 17:20

The Source of All Light and Love

Every aspect of Heaven was bathed in and radiating the light of God. One of the striking things that remains with me is that there is no such thing as darkness or shadows in Heaven. There is no darkness in God. Light expresses the heart and very nature of God. On my return to life in my physical body I was aware of a grayness and lack of the brilliant colors I had experienced in Heaven. My eyes and soul became accustomed to the light of God.

> The light of God in each of us caused the angels to bow to me— to us.

This has changed the way I see life. I try to see the light of God in each person regardless of station or status in life. The light of God in each of us caused the angels to bow to me—to us. In the light of God there is no pretense; there is only love.

Read and Reflect

> *This is the message we have heard from Him and announce to you, that God is Light, and in Him there is no darkness at all.*[6]

God of Joy

Everything in Heaven radiated not only the light and love of God, but also joy. Joy was defined as "living on the edge of a huge laugh." What a description. The Source of my joy is assurance of God's caring for me removing me from the worry of the stuff of daily life. It's not that these things are not important; it is that they are now submerged beneath the care of God. Living in joy is like riding my beautiful horse under the brilliant Canadian sky. There is the sense that I am being carried along. The

---

6 1 John 1:5

joy has crept into the little things of life—the joy of my marriage, the joy of common things like breathing the air on a crisp winter's day or breathing, period! Each day is an unfolding of knowing that God has my life in hand. God is the God of joy.

Read and Reflect

> *You will make known to me the path of life; in Your presence is fullness of joy; in Your right hand there are pleasures forever.*[7]

God of Now

I think most folks tend to live in the past or the future, in either regret or worry. Heaven and God are focused on the "now." The time and dimensions of Heaven all seemed to be focused on the present moment. Things that we would see as having physical distance here on earth were within my grasp just for the reaching. I could see a single flower on the side of a mountain that we might see as miles away. All of the sensory aspects, colors, smells, sounds were all merged together in a concert filling every sense in the present moment of eternity. Eternity seemed to be the eternal now. There is no regret or holdover from the past nor is there a worry of the future. Though God lives in the present moment with us, there is nothing lost. God hears and regards each thought and prayer of our hearts as valuable. Nothing is lost. There are no lost prayers, no lost babies, no lost tears, no lost acts of kindness. All are present and eternal with God. Every aspect of Heaven wrapped me with a blanket of God's intimate love for me. God is the God of now.

> There are no lost prayers, no lost babies, no lost tears, no lost acts of kindness.

---

7 Psalm 16:11

Read and Reflect

I am with you always, even to the end of the age. [8]

God Brings Us to Rest in Himself

My experiences in Heaven communicated the love of God to me in a multi-sensory way, so much so that it penetrated my life deeply. In fact, I had to die to truly live. The experiences revealed God and Jesus Christ, His Son, as my friend, heroically gracious, compassionate, a God of the impossible, the source of love and joy, and One who is present with us at every moment. All of these led me to rest in God.

> His yoke is characterized by humility and gentleness. It is a yoke that is not a burden nor a constraint.

Though I can tell the story, there will be no greater evidence of its truthfulness than my own coming to rest in Jesus Christ. Rest that felt like I had found the home I had always longed for. The longing remains with me constantly—it gets me out of bed each day; it motivates me to share what I experienced. Now this same longing is with me when I sit alongside those in transition to Heaven themselves.

The best way for me to understand and express the rest I've entered into is to say that there was an exchange of yokes in my life. Where I had the yoke, the control column of an aircraft in my grasp from an early age, now the yoke of Jesus came upon me. It meant that God was now leading me. His yoke is characterized by humility and gentleness. It is a yoke that is not a burden nor a constraint. It is a yoke of walking together with Jesus under a yoke of love. It is not a yoke of more stuff or striving. It is a yoke that will not wear out. At the risk of repeating myself, it is a yoke of friendship, grace, compassion, hospitality, love, joy, and constant presence.

---

8 Matthew 28:20

There is no way to conclude this book as my experience continues to unfold with change in my heart and life, making me more His son. I am not a Bible scholar nor a preacher. But I am one who has caught a glimpse of Heaven that will forever change me. My experience in Heaven was not about me; it was about God. I pray that my journey will bring you the hope of Heaven as you continue your own journey until we all see Jesus Christ, face to face—our *Constant Friend.*

> *Come to Me, all who are weary and heavy-laden, and I will give you rest. Take My yoke upon you and learn from Me, for I am gentle and humble in heart, and you will find rest for your souls. For My yoke is easy and My burden is light.*[9]

---

9 Matthew 11:28-30

Notes

CHAPTER TWELVE

The Exchanged Life

It is impossible to stand in a hurricane and not get your hair rearranged. That might describe the effect of the experience I had in Heaven. Every cell of my body, every thought of my mind, the very purpose of living every day has been altered in the hurricane of God's loving presence. I am being rearranged day by day.

God has healed my body from the disease I suffered prior to my experience with Jesus. It has gone missing since my return from Heaven. Curiously, the doctors say that I still have the protein indicating Guillain-Barré in my body, but I have no symptoms of it. I have no pain or paralysis except for the fact that I'm chronologically challenged (older). I need nothing stronger than aspirin now and then for normal wear and tear of life in this unglorified body. In fact, my general health and energy are great.

My personal experience in Heaven with the angels and in the presence of Jesus has altered the way I look at life in a few main areas—how I see God, how I see myself, how I see you, and how I see life in general.

How I See Myself

I wrote of this in an earlier chapter—that my experience revealed the love and character of God—but it has also profoundly changed the way I see myself and my life in general. I have looked into the eyes of Jesus seeing His kindness. It is impossible to look into the eyes of people without remembering the eyes of Jesus. I am learning to see with His eyes.

Perhaps the greatest area of growth in me is compassion for people. People can seem like just part of the landscape to us. Relating to people can be like driving on a road that we've driven on so many times that we begin to tune it out of our consciousness. The problem is that we miss so much of life by just driving through it. I now see myself as one who is filled with the life I found in the eyes of Jesus.

> I'm just a man who has gotten a glimpse of its glory now wishing to share it with a lonesome and weary world.

As the angels revealed the light of God in me, I see myself as loved by God. I am full rather than empty. There is a painting I have seen many times of Jesus standing at a door and knocking that reflects a statement in the Scriptures. I had seen the picture many times but never knew its biblical source or personal meaning for me.[1] Indeed, Jesus came knocking at the door of my heart throughout my life. He kept on knocking until I saw Him face to face. I have opened the door and invited Him to come in and sit at the table with me.

The influence of Jesus extends to every part of my life. I am learning to walk in the love I saw in His eyes. I now read the Bible on a regular basis, not just to master the text but as a reminder and reflection of the love I found that permeated everything in Heaven. I am not a preacher nor

---

1 A painting called "The Light of the World" inspired by Revelation 3:20, "Behold I stand at the door and knock," by William Holman Hunt, 1853.

prophet nor expert on Heaven. I'm just a man who has gotten a glimpse of its glory now wishing to share it with a lonesome and weary world.

How I See Other People

I can see you! I can see the light of God in you. People are not machines to be used in our lives; they are precious and filled with the light of God. How can we ignore that? I am growing in the ability to accept people as Jesus does, just as they are and without judgement. The love and connection I feel for people I meet can now be overwhelming. There are no incidental people. We are all created on purpose with a purpose.

> If you took all the countless billions of acts of kindness, helping the sick, caring for the elderly, loving your sister, loving your brother, helping your pastor, being part of a Christian community, it would be overwhelming.

With this vision of people, I am growing in the ability to feel the pain people experience in their human hearts. I can sense pain because I'm seeing them. The depth of hurt they carry with them. I have an urge to quiet their hearts, to set them at ease in the love of God, to let them know that they are seen and valued—that they bear the light of God.

I had a conversation with one of the angels I have not previously mentioned in this book. I said, "On earth I wake up in the morning and see the news of the carnage the night before. There is so much hatred and killing and murder and disgrace going on. Why hasn't God come back and claimed the earth as He promised?"

The angel looked at me with a wise and quizzical smile and replied, "God isn't finished with the earth yet."

I said, "How can He not be finished? Doesn't He see what happens every day in that mess down there? Why wouldn't He fix it?"

He raised his hand to calm me down, and he said, "James, what mankind fails to realize are the countless acts of kindness that occur every second of every minute of every hour of every earth day." And then he made a motion with his hands, spreading them out before me as if to showcase something. He said, "If you took all the countless billions of acts of kindness, helping the sick, caring for the elderly, loving your sister, loving your brother, helping your pastor, being part of a Christian community, it would be overwhelming. They are all recorded in the book of your life. Then if you took all the evil in the world that you think is so dominant, it is this big." (He made a gesture pinching his thumb and index finger closer together to show me how small the evil is in proportion.)

When we realize that we carry the light of God in us, there is no more need to live to accumulate things. We are no longer self-absorbed people struggling to impress people; we are loved by God and that is impressive enough. When we know we are loved we can walk in the same simple humility as Jesus did on earth, who knew He was loved by His Father.

How I See Life

Life used to be this gray thing I trudged through on a daily basis trying to get ahead or stay ahead of the other guys. Life is now filled with joy. I can live on the edge of a hearty laugh as the angel said. I have seen the effect this story has on the people who hear it. There is a noticeable sense of hope and joy as people hear my story of Heaven. The story gives hearers the reality of something more than the grind—a tangible sense of hope for what is to come. Not only that, but tangible evidence of transformation in the here and now as we experience the love of God. Hundreds of people have told me they sense a peace and tranquility when they stand close to me or hug me. They come back to hear me time after time to experience that feeling. I am humbled by this, but the truth is, it's not me.

A trace of the serenity of Heaven and the goodness of God has somehow traveled with me back to earth. I feel it every day.

I recall a conversation with a 90-year-old doctor who, when hearing the story, looked back on his 60-year medical practice recalling the goodness of God he had seen countless times. The trail of loving care behind him was now evidence of the love before him in eternity.

There is an exchange that has taken place and given me a new purpose and mission for life. Since engaging my mission to tell of my experience in Heaven I have been called to the bedsides of many people in transition to Heaven. As I tell them of the wonders of Heaven, the angels, and the face of Jesus, there is a peace that comes upon them. I can tell them what to expect or what to look for. Sometimes telling the story has brought the dying into a closer relationship with Jesus and allowed them to accept Jesus' offer for those who are weary to come to Him, and in those final hours of life to find faith in Him.

> A trace of the serenity of Heaven and the goodness of God has somehow traveled with me back to earth. I feel it every day.

There has been an exchange of life for me in this experience. There is also one for you as you come to know Jesus Christ and all the wonders that await us all in Heaven but are also ours in the here and now as we give our lives to Jesus Christ.

Take the Journey

As we are restored in God there are several changes that take place. These remind me of Jim's description of the effect of his story on himself as well as those who have experienced Heaven through his story. Read the collection of divine exchanges that are ours as we live under the reign of Christ's hand. I included the whole passage so that you could see where the exchanges came from.

> *The Spirit of the Sovereign Lord is upon me,*
> *for the Lord has anointed me*
> *to bring good news to the poor.*
> *He has sent me to comfort the brokenhearted*
> *and to proclaim that captives will be released*
> *and prisoners will be freed.*
> *He has sent me to tell those who mourn*
> *that the time of the Lord's favor has come,*
> *and with it, the day of God's anger against their enemies.*
> *To all who mourn in Israel,*
> *he will give a crown of beauty for ashes,*
> *a joyous blessing instead of mourning,*
> *festive praise instead of despair.*
> *In their righteousness, they will be like great oaks*
> *that the Lord has planted for his own glory.*[2]

Further Reflection

Notice the exchanges in these verses. Jesus also quoted this passage found in the Gospel of Luke. His mission is our mission—to share the good news, to comfort the brokenhearted, to escort people out of the

---

2 Isaiah 61:1-3, NLT

darkness and set them free from hopelessness, to comfort those who are mourning and tell them they are favored or loved by God. In exchange, we receive beauty instead of ashes, joy instead of mourning, praise instead of despair.

Prayer

Lord Jesus. I thank You for the exchanges I have in You. Let me bring the comfort of Your presence and love to the brokenhearted. Let Your life through me be a light that brings people out of hopelessness. Let me bring comfort to those who have experienced loss and walk with them through life's struggles. Let my life be one of joy and praise as I trust in Your love for me. For Your glory, amen.

Notes

CHAPTER THIRTEEN

It's Not Too Late

Thom's Reflection

*My life began like any other man held
beneath a mother's loving gaze
Somewhere between now and then I
lost the man I could have been
Took everything that wasn't mine to take
but Love believes that it is not too late
Only one of us deserves this cross, a
suffering that should belong to me
Deep within this man I hang beside is the
place where shame and grace collide
And it's beautiful agony that He
believes it's not too late for me.*[1]

---

1 Steven Curtis Chapman, "How Love Wins," Music Inspired by The Story (Capital Christian Music, EMI Christian Music Group, Inc., Word Entertainment LLC, Provident Label Group, 2011).

Six words ushered a man from a pickup truck to the glory of Heaven and the face of Jesus Christ: "God, forgive me—God help me." There was not much of a trail of faithful service or religious practice behind him. There was not much evidence to build a case for salvation from a file of good works. How then can it be that this man would see Heaven let alone stand face to face with Jesus Christ, our constant Friend? It would be fair to ask—how could any of us do so?

My interest in this story began in a conversation at a lunch table with a man I had never met and resulted in helping to write a book I never intended to write. The thing that brought us together culminating in this book was the evidence of sincere and ongoing conversion in the life of a retired pilot who had an amazing experience. He was and is no systematic theologian. He is a fellow "ragamuffin," to use Brennan Manning's term. As Michael W. Smith wrote in the Foreword for Manning's *Ragamuffin Gospel*, "We are all ragamuffins, and we are all endlessly wrapped in God's arms of grace."[2] In a word, the point of this story, like all of our stories who have the hope of experiencing all Jim has experienced, is grace—a radical life-catching, destiny-transforming, unearned, and scandalously free grace. A grace that says, *It's not too late!*

Some may be uneasy with this kind of grace and search the Scriptures for where we should draw the line before we get into the realm of "sloppy agape" or "greasy grace." Maybe they would ask, "Just how far can we go on grace until it becomes license? Is grace just a "get out of Hell free card?" As the apostle Paul put it, "What shall we say then? Are we to continue in sin so that grace may increase? May it never be!"[3] Nonetheless, grace says, *"It's not too late."*

As I became familiar with Jim's life story, I was reminded of another man who struggled until he had a life-changing conversion—John

---

2 Brennen Manning, *The Ragamuffin Gospel: Good News for the Bedraggled, Beat-Up, and Burnt Out* (Colorado Springs: Multnomah Books, 2008), 8.
3 Romans 6:1-2

Newton. Newton was the composer of the well-known hymn "Amazing Grace." Newton's mother passed away when he was very young, though she gave him a spiritual basis from which to live. Newton's father was a sea captain and was seldom home, so Newton grew up without a consistent fathering influence. John Newton went through years searching for peace, trying to find it in carnal pleasures. He experienced many ups and downs in his early life, nearly being hung for desertion from the British Navy at one point. He was a man searching for meaning and peace in the stuff of life. To the world, Newton was very successful man, but inside he was filled with doubt and fear.

Eventually Newton became the captain of a ship transporting slaves from Africa. One night there was a terrible storm from which Newton believed they would not survive. He cried out for himself and the passengers of his ship in the midst of the storm, and somehow God miraculously saved the ship. This drama was the beginning of Newton's conversion culminating in his repentance from the slave trade and turning to Christ.[4] Though John Newton piloted slave ships for many years, the amazing grace of God met him in the midst of a raging storm. Grace said, *It's not too late.*

Conversion

In Jim's account, his journey to Heaven and to the heart of God began when he cried out, "God, forgive me." This, though thin, was an act of acknowledging that Jim could not save or help himself. It was an act of repentance and conversion. Repentance is turning away from our old way to God. Wayne Grudem defined conversion this way: "Conversion is a single action of turning from sin in repentance and turning to Christ

---

4 Based on the book by Jonathan Aitken, *John Newton, from Disgrace to Amazing Grace* (Wheaton, IL: Crossway Books, 2007).

in faith."[5] I will not parse each word of Jim's request for forgiveness and grace. I have seen the fruit of it in a life and relationship with Christ that is growing. Conversion is turning from one power source to another.

Jesus gave us a great illustration of conversion in the gospels when He described growth in the kingdom of God. He said that after a seed was planted in the ground, a blade popped through the soil. Before the seed

> Conversion is moving from a lesser power to the greater power.

comes through the ground it lives off its own resources. Conversion may be compared to a seed popping through the ground to connect with the sun for its further growth through photosynthesis. When it comes through the ground it is connected to the sun, the greater source of power and growth.[6] Conversion is moving from a lesser power to the greater power. This conversion to the greater source requires a turning away from self and toward God. This turning is referred to as repentance.[7]

Is it possible for someone to turn toward Christ in the last possible moments of life and find Heaven? That would require a truly amazing grace. The grace of God brings all of us onto the same level ground. We stand in grace by faith or calling out to God in deep trust. Listen to Paul's description of our standing.

> *Therefore, since we have been made right in God's sight by faith, we have peace with God because of what Jesus Christ our Lord has done for us. Because of our faith, Christ has brought us into this place of undeserved privilege where we*

---

5 Wayne Grudem, *Bible Doctrine; Essential Teaching of the Christian Faith* (Grand Rapids, MI: Zondervan, 1999), 311.

6 Mark 4:26-29

7 Repentance in the Hebrew language is *teshuva,* from the root shuv, which means to turn.

*now stand, and we confidently and joyfully look forward to
sharing God's glory.*[8]

When Jim stood before Christ in Heaven, it was only on the basis
of his calling out to God with his thin request, "God, forgive me," then
"God help me." On that thinnest of requests, Jim saw the greatest glory
of God; His grace said, *It's not too late!*

The Other Cross

Consider the other cross in the gospels. On the day that Jesus was
crucified there were two others crucified along with Him—one on His
right and the other on His left. Read the Bible account:

> *One of the criminals who were hanged there was hurling
> abuse at Him, saying, "Are You not the Christ? Save Yourself
> and us!" But the other answered, and rebuking him said, "Do
> you not even fear God, since you are under the same sentence
> of condemnation? And we indeed are suffering justly, for we
> are receiving what we deserve for our deeds; but this man has
> done nothing wrong." And he was saying, "Jesus, remember
> me when You come in Your kingdom!" And He said to him,
> "Truly I say to you, today you shall be with Me in Paradise."*[9]

I can imagine this man hanging between life and death in agony and
desperate fear next to the King of Kings on that cruel tree. He would be
struggling for every breath, filled with indescribable pain with even the
slightest movement—every breath a reminder that it could be his last.
Then the man's thoughts turned toward the One who bled beside him.
He turned his face toward the crucified Christ. In the midst of his agony
the man on the other cross, the one crucified with Christ, gathered in

8 Romans 5:1-2, NLT
9 Luke 23:39-43

enough breath to issue a final, halting, yet faith-filled request. "Jesus, remember me." The response came without a moment's deliberation from the One who was the incarnation of the Father's love on earth. "Today, you will be with Me in paradise."

Upon what basis was the man on the other cross given the assurance of Heaven? There is no evidence in the account that the man could climb down from his cross to do a few good works. He could not go into a church building and find an altar to speak a formal prayer of salvation. We know of no formal training the man had in the things of God. He had no time to write a tithe check. I'm fairly certain that he could not recite the five points of Calvinism or the Roman's Road to salvation. Is it possible, then, that it is just that simple—that a man called out in desperate agony and guilt to Christ and was saved? He will be in the same Heaven as, say, the apostle Paul or Martin Luther? I realize that many readers may find this offensive to think that it could be just that simple—that the man on the other cross was "saved" on such a thin basis. Grace is initiated on the thinnest request of man for the greatest glory of God. Grace said, *It's not too late.*

> He turned his face toward the crucified Christ. In the midst of his agony the man on the other cross, the one crucified with Christ, gathered in enough breath to issue a final, halting, yet faith-filled request.

Grace puts us all on equal ground. It is the sole means of salvation. This does not mean universalism—that everyone is automatically in. There is the necessity for conviction of sin, repentance (turning toward Christ in faith), resulting in conversion, leading to justification based on the blood of Jesus Christ alone.

The man on the other cross recognized his sin by telling the other "criminal" that he deserved death (conviction). Then he turned toward Jesus (repentance), recognizing that Jesus was the King, and then, in faith, called out that Jesus would "remember" him (confession of faith).

Jesus responded to his faithful request and took his sin upon Himself, and that day the man on the other cross saw the same paradise Jim saw.

The calling out of the man on the other cross was a desperate call, just like Jim who was passing away in the cab of his truck. It was a desperate cry coming from a deep awareness of the distance between himself and the kingdom of God. In that final moment, invited by the Spirit of God deep within him, Jim turned toward God. "Turn to Me and be saved, all the ends of the earth; for I am God, and there is no other."[10]

> Grace puts us all on equal ground. It is the sole means of salvation.

The words of Steven Curtis Chapman's song, "How Love Wins," express the words of the man who was crucified with Jesus Christ and give expression to what happened to one man who went from pickup truck to the glory of Heaven and who now tells his brothers and sisters of the wonders shown him in Heaven.

Further Reflection

Read these words slowly and reflect on your own need for the grace that says, *It's not too late.*

> *My life began like any other man held*
> *beneath a mother's loving gaze*
> *Somewhere between now and then I*
> *lost the man I could have been*
> *Took everything that wasn't mine to take*
> *but Love believes that it is not too late*
> *Only one of us deserves this cross, a*
> *suffering that should belong to me*

---

10 Isaiah 45:22

Deep within this man I hang beside is the
place where shame and grace collide
And it's beautiful agony that He believes
it's not too late for me.[11]

Our entrance into the kingdom of Heaven comes as we realize our need and turn our heads toward the cross of Christ, remembering that Jesus is the King and asking Him to remember us. It's not too late for us to turn toward Christ now.

- Is there a deep longing for peace in your heart? *It's not too late.*

- Does your heart need healing from past sins and mistakes? *It's not too late.*

- Maybe you are saying, "I've never been a religious person or served God." *It's not too late.*

- Maybe your life is caught up in some kind of snare or a tangled mess. *It's not too late.*

- Maybe you've lived in your own strength and haven't found purpose in life. *It's not too late.*

- Maybe you've gone to church all of your life but never really connected with the heart of Jesus Christ. *It's not too late.*

- Maybe while you've been reading this book you've become aware of a longing for Heaven and the face of Jesus Christ in your heart. *It's not too late.*

- Whatever the deep need or longing is in your heart, the Lord says, *"It's not too late."*

---

11 Chapman, "How Love Wins."

Prayer

*Jesus, I realize that I have tried to live my own life my way. I've missed Your best for my life. I admit to You now that I cannot make it on my own anymore, and I confess that I have sinned and don't deserve Heaven. I'm tired of trying to prove myself to You and to the world. I ask You now to save and heal me and give me the grace to become like You. I thank You for loving me—for inviting me to love You back. I choose to live for You now and will stand in Your presence one day in Heaven to praise You forever. I thank you that **it's not too late** for me. I pray this in Your precious name, Lord Jesus. Amen.*

Notes

About Jim Woodford

James Woodford was born in Newfoundland, Canada. Losing his father when he was two years old, James grew up in the home of his maternal grandparents. James developed a fascination with aircraft at an early age, as there was a seaplane dock at the edge of the river where the family lived. James became one of the youngest licensed pilots in Canada with a flying career that began at age 19. James flew small aircraft to the remote lakes in the provinces as other routes were generally not available, especially in the rugged winters. He gradually worked his way up to fly larger aircraft until he became captain of a major airline. Having flown from Toronto to Timbuktu, James was well traveled. James also has a love for horses and now resides in New Brunswick, Canada with his wife Lorraine and several horses. James travels in North and South America encouraging the body of Christ with his account of his experience in Heaven, and he also has been a comfort to families of those who have lost loved ones assuring them of the glories of Heaven and the love of God in Jesus Christ.

For more about
Jim Woodford

www.jimwoodford.com

www.facebook.com/pg/Jim-Woodford

About Thom Gardner

Thom Gardner has ministered as a Bible teacher or pastor since 1986 and is now President of Restored Life Ministries, Inc., a ministry dedicated to holistic spiritual formation. He travels internationally to equip leaders throughout the body of Christ by leading retreats and training seminars using his techniques of interactive encounter with the presence of Christ through the Scriptures. He has authored several books, including *Healing the Wounded Heart, Relentless Love, Living the God-Breathed Life, The Healing Journey,* and *Everything that Grows.*

For more about
Thom Gardner and Restored Life Ministries, Inc

What we do—
www.restoredlifeministries.com/events

Why we do what we do—
www.restoredlifeministries.com/services

Resources—
www.restoredlifeministries.com/resources

OTHER BOOKS AND RESOURCES
BY
DR. THOM GARDNER

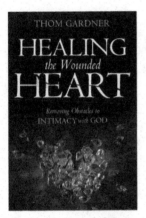

Healing the Wounded Heart
9780768423266

The Healing Journey
9780768432305

Relentless Love
9780768441031

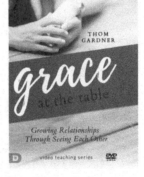

Living the God-Breathed Life
9780768436198

Grace at the Table DVD
88500766090

VISIT HTTPS://WWW.RESTOREDLIFEMINISTRIES.COM/RESOURCES